ASSASSINS OBEY THE QURAN

*Christine Tasin
& René d'Armor*

*Cover design: digital picture
Jean-Louis Chollet 2017*

Association Résistance Républicaine
101 avenue du Général Leclerc –
75685 PARIS CEDEX 14
FRANCE

ISBN 978-2-9546379-2-1
September 2017
All rights reserved

Without limiting the rights under copyright reserved above, no part of this publication may be reproduced, stored in or introduced into a retrieval system, or transmitted, in any form, or by any means (electronic, mechanical, photocopying, recording, or otherwise), without the prior written permission of both the copyright owner and the above publisher of this book.

"Man must retain the power to resist, to oppose, to say no. He then has no excuse. Too many go whichever way the wind blows. Their acts, disjointed and piecemeal, no longer make sense."

"Les Sentinelles du soir" (1999 – French only)

Hélie Denoix de Saint Marc (1922-2013)
French Resistant in WWII
Major in the French Foreign Legion

By the same author *(French only)*

Les Assises de l'islamisation de nos pays
By Pierre Cassen et Christine Tasin - 2011 Editions Riposte Laïque

La Faute du Bobo Jocelyn
By Pierre Cassen et Christine Tasin – 2011 Editions Riposte Laïque

Qu'est-ce qu'elle vous a fait la République ?
By Christine Tasin - 2013 Editions Résistance Républicaine

Contents

Warning 8
Foreword by René Marchand 10
PART 1 14
Why have Muslims Martyrized us for 1400 years? 14
Chapter 1 17
The history of Islam, a long succession of terrorist acts 17
A) The beginnings of Islam 17
B) The conquest... 18
C) The martyrdom of Europe 20
Chapter 2 23
Terrorism is in the Quran and the Hadiths of Muhammad .. 23
A) Hatred towards non-Muslims is omnipresent in the sacred Muslim texts 23
B) Islam is a religion of peace and love which has nothing to do with Merah and other murderers. 27
Conclusion 33
There is Muslim and Muslim, fortunately 33
PART 2 36
The Quran and the United States of America 36
Introduction: Quran, Hadiths, Sunnah… 37
Chapter 1 38
U.S. Constitution & Law versus Sharia Law 38
1. Freedom of Religion 39
2. Freedom of Speech 41

3. Freedom of Thought 42
4. Freedom of Artistic Expression 45
5. Freedom of the Press 47
6. No Equality of the People 47
7. No equal protection 49
8. No Equal Rights for Women 53
9. Women Can Be Beaten 58
10. A non-Muslim Cannot Bear Arms 58
11. There is No Democracy in Islam 59
12. Our Constitution is a Man-made Document of Ignorance
.... 60
13. Non-Muslims are Third-class Citizens 60
14. All Governments must be ruled by Sharia law 61
15. Sharia is not interpretative 62
16. There is no Golden Rule 63
Islamic law and American law 64
   Chapter 2 67
The Quran, a Manual of Hate & War 67
   Chapter 3 76
Jihad 76
The three stages of Jihad 81
   Epilogue 87
   URGENT ACTIONS 89

Warning

Why this book? Most of us are still not aware of this imminent danger. The Medias, as always, are massaging the mind of the "tolerant", the "ignorant" or the "politically correct"… the only escape, for some of us, regrettably resulting too often in complete disinterest.

Islam, since its inception, had one direct order, CONQUER THE WORLD FOR ALLAH! Today Islam, the Muslims, are finally well on their way to do just that. Originated in the Middle East, Islam has spread into the Orient, the African continent, Europe and here in America. The Quran establishes the step-by-step invasion process. First a stealth "peaceful" subversion into the target State institutions, while building a network of mosques and prayer centers. Never forget this quote when you see a mosque, *"The mosques are our barracks, the domes our helmets, the minarets our bayonets and the faithful our soldiers."*
- (Recep Tayyip Erdogan – Turkey's President – 1998.)

All the things and actions that Muslims must do are found in the Holy Book of Islam: the Quran, and in other Islamic documents.

Thereafter, as the number of Muslims grows and traction takes hold, the Quran commands the request of more and more special privileges to continue the irreversible social integration. The Quran then orders to increase the fecundity rate with multiple wives and enslaved concubines to increase their critical numbers and prepare for the final stretch: outright war and global violent takeover! The Islamic law, the Sharia, will supplant all constitutional orders of mankind as ordered "directly by Allah" in his war manual, the Quran.

This book is a factual data record of the spread and growth of Islam in the World, as we observe, today. No fiction, no unverifiable claims, just the simple facts as anyone can verify through thousands of Internet sources by reading verses of the "Holy Quran".

This book's objective is to inform the American public about today's state of affairs and to encourage the American people to witness this increasingly fast spreading ideology right into our everyday lives. Soon you will know about this ultimate danger and be appalled by the facts. So, if and when things get worse, you won't say: "I did not know!"

Friends, Patriots and Countrymen, promote this book, because:

THE "LAND OF THE FREE" IS IN GREAT DANGER.

We sincerely thank you.

Christine Tasin and René d'Armor

Foreword by René Marchand

The book by Christine Tasin and René d'Armor reminds us of three realities that our politicians, journalists, intellectuals, parish priests, rabbis, freemasons ... of "dominant thought" are trying to conceal from our fellow citizens:

- *Terrorism is in the genetics of Islam.* Suffice it to quote - and the authors do it very well - the countless Surats of the Quran calling for violence against non-Muslims, and Hadiths - the collections of facts and sayings of Allah's envoy - who tell us how this envoy, of which the Quran is the "beautiful model", used robbery, torture, deportation, ethnic cleansing, enslavement, assassination, rape, massacre ... to impose its autocracy. The Quran and Hadiths are the source of the Muslim Law, Sharia, which legalizes behaviors in our most criminal eyes when they are fulfilled "in the way of Allah".

- *Throughout history, Muslims have constantly used terrorism*, as well as all other forms of violence. They also made widespread use of lying, concealing truth, cunning: the taqiyya, justified, as it should be, by the Quran and the example of Muhammad. Throughout history, Muslim societies have always lived for war - war booty is a gift of Allah, according to the Quran - and for the exploitation of peoples enslaved by terror. Muslims discontinued their assault on others only when they were dominated or contained.

- *Islam will not change.* The founding principle of Islamic civilization, the Sunnah, which bases legal and moral legitimacy on the past and condemns innovation, forbids any distancing from the Quran and the Hadiths. The natural movement of Islam is not evolution, but involution, the return to the past, and precisely the past, more or less mythicized, of earlier times.

It must be known that there never was and never will be any Reformation in Islam (or else by force, like an Atatürk, and for how long?). We have to face up to the danger we are facing.

"Radicalization", which we are seeing everywhere, in Muslim countries as in our suburbs (at least in Europe, so far), is well on its way to last a long, long time.

"Radicalization" is not apart from Islam. It is strict respect for Islamic law. Through this law, which deals with all the moments of a human life, Muslims are from childhood confined, enclosed, in a network of obligations and prohibitions, but also prejudices. Nowadays, Muslims who have fled Islam confirm having been subjected to brainwashing from a very young age. And among these constituent elements of the Muslim mentality, yesterday and today, there is and will always be the hatred of non-Muslims, and the sacred duty of fighting them at all costs.

Westerners do not want to see Islam such as it is. They invented "Islamism", which would be a denaturing of Islam for political purposes, as if Islam was not itself political. In France, our leaders are striving to find "valid interventionists" to set up a French-style Islam compatible with French values. To gain a few more years of relative tranquility, these tremblers are ready for all complacency, for all "reasonable accommodations". At the same time, to please the enemy, they do not hesitate to drag before the courts the Resistants who reveal the true nature of Islam (by the way, how many complaints against ChristineTasin?)

The few politicians who, far from microphones and cameras, admit that they recognize the threat, add quickly and pathetically: "Yes, but what can we do?"

We must answer this question bluntly: "We are at war, you say. So, this war, let's have it! And first by designating the enemy: Islam, taking it as it is and acting accordingly."

Immediately, we must say, proclaim, spread everywhere this truth: Islam is not a religion. And this is demonstrated. What do we mean by "religion" today? A faith, which belongs to the private sphere of each individual, including various rites and practices that do not disturb the public order in any way. Islam is something quite different. It is a Law, which totally governs the lives of believers and must be imposed on all mankind. In France, legislation on religions was outlined by law in December 1905. Islam is outside the scope of this law, and article 1 reads: "The Republic ensures freedom of conscience." Islam refuses freedom of conscience: a Muslim cannot leave Islam under penalty of death, a Muslim child will be necessarily Muslim with the same prohibition,
a Muslim cannot marry a non-Muslim, and so on.

With this trap-word "religion", we tolerate, by spirit of tolerance, intolerance. We give an expansionist and warlike totalitarianism every license to deploy on our soil, to build its advanced bastions, its centers of formation and propaganda; we allow its political commissioners to indulge, indoctrinate, judge, punish, recruit, and organize massacres...

The first duty of men and women who claim to rule the West, of all shades and degrees, is to take note of the fact that Islam is, in fact, outside American, French, and numerous Occidental laws. It must therefore be controlled and repressed, or even prohibited pure and simple. To begin with, at the legislative level, it must be given a legal qualification that is precise and in conformity with reality, so that the magistrates are finally obligated to put an end to their misdeeds. Terrorism is inscribed in the Quran and provides the elements of the record in superabundance, clearly and irrefutably.

I say to the readers of this book which, in a small format, contains the essential part of what must be known about our enemy: "Have these few pages read to the ignorant, to the naive, but also to your elected leaders. Based on facts and quotations, call these traitors, by word, with letters or emails, or by manifesting. Bore them in a thousand ways. Make life difficult for them. Constrain them from getting out of their lies and their silences of cowards. In the fight against Islam, where peace in the West, the future of our children, our way of life, our civilization as a whole are played. You have, with this little book, a weapon. It is your duty and your honor, but also in your best interest, to use it. "

Through their words, Christine Tasin and René d'Armor tell us: Let's act!

PART 1

Why have Muslims Martyrized us for 1400 years?

By Christine Tasin

Stabbings, decapitations, cars running over pedestrians, bombings or Kalashnikov attacks ... The terror unleashed by a few Muslim fanatics wins in Europe and especially France. Who says terror says terrorism. Unlike traditional wars, which, despite their horrors, follow a certain code of conduct, including respect for civilian populations and prisoners of war, Islamic terrorism, like all terrorism, creates a war that has not been formally declared and targets, at least in France and lately in Germany, almost exclusively non-Muslim groups and individuals. This is how France is explicitly targeted by the jihadists of the Islamic state: *"Explode France, reduce France to crumbs, explode the heads of these kafirs"*. *"In the same way that they allow themselves to strike our sisters, in the same way that they permit themselves to make illicit what Allah has made lawful, in the same way that they prevent our sisters from putting the niqab on. Explode their heads, explode their heads, whether with a stone or whatever... If you cannot get a pistol, there are stones, there are knives, it is necessary"*. *"Take the example of our brother Mohamed Merah (a 23-year-old French petty criminal of Algerian descent, self-styled al Qaeda jihadist accused of killing seven people, died in a hail of bullets on March 23, 2012), make an example of him and blow up their heads, kill them, kill them, wherever they are, kill them, do not let them live in peace, since they do not allow our brothers to live in peace today."*[1]

Everyone knows what that means. It is a question of imposing on all, through fear, death and suffering, the law of Allah (Sharia) by trampling the rights of freedom to think, to speak, to choose his government; by refusing democracy and debate. It is clear that we have moved on to the ultimate stage of terrorism; it is no longer a matter of obtaining the release of Palestinian terrorists in exchange for halting the attacks or the recognition of Palestine as was the case in the 1970s or 1980s.

No more claims, just a cry "Allah Akbar "(God is great) and the terrorists do their dirty work.

Everyone expects our country to sink into horror and desolation, but the interpretations of the phenomenon diverge. For some, these people are coming only from the extremist fringe, more or less unbalanced individuals having nothing to do with Islam that would be only "peace and love", while others, of whom we are, see in the burning news of France the resurgence of a violent past and Muslim conqueror and the *stricto sensu* application of the two compulsory references in terms of Islam, the Quran and the Hadiths which constitute the "Sunnah" The life of Muhammad. This is what we will endeavor to demonstrate by first relying on the history of Islam and its proselytes before showing to what sacred texts precisely the acts of terrorism are linked and the terrorists obey.

[1] http://www.europe-israel.org/2014/12/letat-islamique-en-francais-dans-une-nouvelle-video-faites-exploser- la-france-reduisez-la-france-en-miettes-explosez-leurs-tetes/

Chapter 1

The history of Islam, a long succession of terrorist acts

A) The beginnings of Islam

We will not recall here how or why a simple camel driver leaving Mecca, where he does not have the position he feels he deserves after the death of his rich and elderly wife, finds himself in Medina, attacking convoys and developing a new religion. This is not the subject of this article, and we shall refer to the specialists who have written exciting works on the subject.[2]

What interests us is the beginnings of Muslim proselytism. Muhammad and his small group of Muslims vegetated in misery in Medina for more than a year until they decided to escape by brigandage and raiding, practices that are traditional in what René Marchand calls "*The Arab tradition of the desert*" (see note 2, *Reconquista*). In 624 they attack a caravan during the sacred truce of the pilgrimages to the Kaaba, with all impunity. After this act, Muhammad receives a revelation from Allah, who justifies his actions... He brings together more than three hundred men attracted to this fearless man pretending to act in the name of Allah, who stripped the Great Caravan (mounted by the Meccans once a year) which was without an armed escort...

From that time on, Muhammad is the undisputed leader of the Muslims, and he will use and abuse violence, bringing terror wherever he passes. Assassination of a woman poet who mocked him, of another poet, an old centenarian man; Ethnic cleansing of Medina from which the Jews are hunted; Genocide of the Jewish tribe of the Banu Qurayza whose entire male population, including adolescents, is slaughtered in the public square...

Thus, through terror, Muhammad has shown to all that he will not shrink from anything to impose his law, and the verses inciting violence multiply in the Quran. War is a duty imposed by Allah and everyone must participate in it, either as a warrior or as a contributor to the war effort, and each will receive his reward after death in Paradise and receive his share of the booty. It is indeed booty, the property of others ripped off by violence, the proceeds of the sale of women and taxes imposed on non-Muslims in the conquered cities, and this will be true everywhere, throughout the history of Islam that will follow.

2. - *The Foundations of Islam. Between writing and history.* Alfred-Louis de Prémare. Tetrahedron 2004
- *Mohammed Counter-Investigation.* René Marchand. Editions of the Echiquier - 2006
- *Unmasked Islam.* Lagartempe, Editions de Paris - 2007
- *The beginnings of the Arab-Muslim conquests. Myths and Realities*, by Louis Chagnon - Godefroy de Bouillon - 2007
- *Reconquista,* by René Marchand. Editions Riposte laïque - 2013

B) The conquest

The Sunnah, or "life of Muhammad," imposes identification with the prophet and therefore the application of the laws and rules dictated to him by Allah. Therefore, after his death, his disciples will not cease to conquer the countries surrounding them, going farther and farther, to transform the unbelieving lands and very often Christian lands into lands of Allah and enrich themselves there in passing without needing to work.

"Therefore, from 634 to 647, under the first three caliphs, the Muslims seized the lands of Byzantium from Syria to Tripolitania and they put down the Persian Empire," says René Marchand in Reconquista.

In Yarmouk, in August 636, *"Blood flowed like a river,"* says Tabari, *"there would have been 120,000 dead on the Christian side during the battle, and 40,000 Christians would have been killed in the following days. Those figures may be exaggerated, but they give an idea of the armed masses involved, the roughness of the fighting and the ferocious character of the massacres of civilians."* Louis Chagnon (quoted note 2).

"In 651, Persia was completely conquered, as were all the eastern provinces of Byzantium, Damascus, Jerusalem and Alexandria, in other words, the whole area that was rightly called the "Fertile crescent." These Middle Eastern countries invaded by Saracen raptors, had been, together, the place of invention and diffusion of technical and cultural advances that have led humankind from the state of nature to the state of culture. It is this immense fruit, cultivated and accumulated over several millennia by societies of laborious producers, which predators Saracens were going to pick up to engulf it in an infernal and perpetual jihad, to the point of drying up the source permanently. War has always been very costly... A few decades of War suffice to ruin a nation; a Saracen war of a century will have sufficed to ruin the legendary fertile Crescent." Laurent Lagartempe (book cited in note 2).

These are the particularities of Islamic wars that could be described as terrorist for the last 1400 years. Violence against the civilian population, the sale of women, the slaughter or emasculation of men, the enslavement of the conquered peoples, the refusal and destruction of what is not Muslim, the permanent tribute demanded of non-Muslims... Where the Saracen troops pass, progress dies away. And if we find, inevitably, such acts in the history of mankind, they are only the punctual fact of men or countries subject to dictators; they are not inherent in a system that applies everywhere, regardless of age, peoples and civilization. Unfortunately for them, the populations of the southern shores of the Mediterranean, conquered, did not reach the Reconquista, unlike Europe.

C) The martyrdom of Europe

Provence? (*Southern Region of France*) Invaded in 734, the whole country, from Arles to Nice, is ravaged.

The ancient and rich Provincia Romana? Corsica? Sardinia? Between the eighth century and the thirteenth century, the Mediterranean shoreline fell into misery and remained there because of the incessant raids of the Saracens, the looting, the destruction of French cities as important as Marseille, Arles, Fréjus, Antibes, Nice or Toulon, the removal of women and children, the murder of men or their sale as slaves... Is it a coincidence that in some of our churches we still find trunks where we put the money necessary for the redemption of the men of the village who had been removed?

Sicily? *"Subjected to the Muslim yoke for two centuries, it suffers the fate of all the countries occupied by the Muslims: the natives are reduced to the condition of dhimmis, that is to say subjected permanently to fiscal and psychological pressures under threat of returning to the state of effective war".* Laurent Lagartempe, (book cited note 2).

But the Saracen exactions have also not spared the interior: the Alps' *défilés*, the Durance or the Verdon valleys. Which region has not undergone Muslim terrorism, its violence and its rapines?

Which country has not suffered Muslim terrorism? Italy, Spain, occupied for 7 centuries, with a Reconquista which lasted nearly 3 centuries; The Byzantine Empire fell in 1453...

Certainly, and fortunately, on several occasions, the Saracens were beaten, obliged to withdraw thanks to the obstinacy and valor of Eudes of Aquitaine in 721, Charles Martel in 732, Godefroy de Bouillon which liberated Jerusalem in 1099 (the crusades, too often forgotten, were never more than answers to jihad, in order to liberate Christian territories and Christians from the Muslim yoke); Everywhere we have had to undertake what Laurent Lagartempe calls "*a merciless war against the perpetual Islamic terrorism.*" (Note 2) And the result is without appeal:

"*The pirate raids were so devastating and so frequent that the rich coastal plains [of France] continued to be deserted from their inhabitants, obliged to organize their survival some distance from the coast in places easier to protect. This withdrawal from the habitat of fertile plains to the mountains was the rule throughout Provence after three centuries of Islamic martyrdom. The human settlements of this period of terror had nothing to do with those of the peaceful and prosperous Provincia Romana; whole territories had returned to wasteland, haunted by wolves, emptied of their inhabitants, massacred, captured, with miserable refugees hiding in the forests. The weight of the previous great Saracen depression definitively sank Provence, and favored a lasting transfer of prosperity from South to North of Western Europe."* Laurent Lagartempe (note 2).

The perpetual wars led to the Battle of Lepanto, which in 1571 saw the victory of the Christian fleet over the Turkish fleet, not to mention Vienna in 1683, which caused the disappearance of the same Turks from Central Europe, and the disembarkation, in what will be the future Algeria, of the French who came in 1830 to put an end to the barbarian raids on the coasts of France.

Muslim history repeats itself, and the commandments of the Quran require that this be the case so long as the whole planet does not become "dar al-islam", land of Islam. This is what we will focus on demonstrating.

[3]. *Chronicle of Tabari, history of the prophets and kings*, Tabari, historian and exegete of the Quran, ninth century.

Chapter 2

Terrorism is in the Quran and the Hadiths of Muhammad

A) Hatred towards non-Muslims is omnipresent in the sacred Muslim texts

First, there is a hatred of non-Muslims in the Quran that should shake anti-racism specialists who feverishly seek hatred of Muslims in the writings of Islamic critics. This hatred is non-existent, because if we fight against Islam, it is first and foremost to protect and free those who, born Muslims, did not choose their religion and risk their lives if ever they choose to distance themselves from it. This is the case in Mauritania of Mohamed Sheikh Ould Mohamed, who was sentenced to death for apostasy on December 24, 2014 for criticizing the social order in his country, which he compared to that prevailing at the time of the Prophet Muhammad.[4]

Mauritania simply applies the Sharia, that is, the precepts of Allah transmitted to the Prophet, in this case the application of a Hadith called Bukhari,[5] foreseeing that the blood of a Muslim cannot be widespread except in three cases, including that of apostasy. *"For one who turns away from Islam and leaves the Muslims"*. Bukhari VXXXIII 17.

This absolute hatred towards non-Muslims no doubt explains why terrorism is consubstantial with Islam; there can be no pity or compassion for one who is considered an enemy and a sub-man *(a "sub-man": a man or a being who has human characteristics in a very inferior degree)*.

Laurent Lagartempe, in another of his works[6], recorded more than 40 verses imprecating unbelievers in Surat 2, called "*La Vache*" (The cow): "*To them the torment, qualified according to the case of unlimited (verses 7; 114), frightful (10, 85, 104, 174), terrible (165, 174), shameful (90, 114) To them the perdition (27), the misfortune. Let them be the hosts of fire (39; 82; 167; 217; 221; 257); combustion (24); furnace (119); Gehenna* (206): they are worthy of the worst insults, they are like monkeys that are rejected (65); dedicated to the curse of God (88, 159, 161), to the wrath of God (61), to the hatred of God (98), to the wrath of Heaven (59), hunt them, fight them, kill them (191, 194, 244.)*"

*In the Hebrew Bible, Gehenna was initially where some of the kings of Judaea sacrificed their children by fire.

And whoever, non-Muslim, submits and pays the dhimmi jizya in Muslim territory must respect Islam and its rules and recognize his inferiority:

4. Express.fr, December 26, 2014
5. Imam Bukhari, of the ninth century, established a collection of Hadiths recognized as a reference by the Sunnites.
6. *A Guide to the Quran*, Consep, 2003

"*When the sacred months (*) are over, slay the idolaters wherever you find them. Arrest them, besiege them, and lie in ambush everywhere for them. If they repent and take to prayer and render the alms levy, allow them to go their way. God is forgiving and merciful.*" Surat 9:5, (The Verse of the Sword).

(*)These four sacred months mentioned in the Quran are not sequential in the Islamic calendar; rather they are spread throughout the year. Thus some scholars believe that

Muhammad gave some of the various pagan groups about one year until he was to make war upon them. Other pagan groups were to experience his aggression earlier, after 4 sequential months.

The Mozarabic (Christians living in the territory of Andalusia under Muslim rule), who dared to criticize Islam and Muhammad, paid the price in the ninth century. They had to choose between escape, conversion to Islam, or death. Exactly the same ultimatum that was given to Iraqi Christians by the Islamic State in the last few months, and that has resulted in numerous executions of Christians, including that of adolescents who refused to convert, as well as the enslavement of women and very young girls, who were sold and raped. We find the reign of terror established by Muhammad in Medina against Jews in particular. It is frightful to recognize this as a perennial issue coming directly from the barbarism of the Middle Ages.

Moreover, incitement to murder infidels abound also in the Quran and the Hadiths and it is likely that the assassinations and other slaughters that have marked the years 2014-2015 and the first half of 2016 are only their application. Western hostages, including the Frenchman Hervé Gourdel (beheaded in Algeria on Sept. 23, 2014) have borne the brunt of this hatred of non-Muslims associated with the desire to impose through terror the compliance to and application of the Sharia, as evidenced by the verses and Hadith below:

"When the Messenger or Allah would cut feet and hands of those who had stolen his camels and that they would remove their eyes with nails heated in the fire, Allah scolded him and revealed: The punishment of those who make war on Allah and His apostle and confront them with all forces on earth will be execution by beheading or crucifixion." (Daoud XXXVIII 4357).

"Your Lord inspired the angels: I am with you, so support those who believe. I will cast terror into the hearts of those who disbelieve. So strike above the necks, and strike off every fingertip of theirs." (Surat 8:12). "That is because they opposed God and His Messenger. Whoever opposes God and His Messenger—God is severe in retribution." (Surat 8:13)

"So when you meet those who disbelieve [in battle], strike [their] necks [behead them], then when you have inflicted slaughter upon them, secure their bonds, and either [confer] favor afterwards or ransom [them] until the war lays down its burdens." (Surat 47:4 – extract)

"Fight them until there is no [more] fitnah and [until] worship is [acknowledged to be] for Allah. But if they cease, then there is to be no aggression except against the oppressors." (Surat 2:193)

"Say to those who disbelieve: if they desist, their past will be forgiven. But if they persist—the practice of the ancients has passed away." (Surat 8:38)

Hervé Gourdel was murdered (Sept 23, 2014, Tikjda, Algeria) because he was an infidel and because it was necessary to frighten the other infidels, to teach them to fear and thus respect Islam. The Western hostages were slaughtered because the Islamic head of state, who claims to be the new caliph, Abu-Bakr-Al-Baghdadi, applies the Quran which allows jihadists to commit acts of cruelty in order to spread terror.

As for looting, expropriation of others and other raids, they are also a Quranic prescription: *"And He caused you to inherit their land and their homes and their properties and a land which you have not trodden. And ever is Allah, over all things, competent."* (Surat 33:27)

Yet, some say, we should not dwell on the sacred texts, which could only be understood and interpreted by Muslim scholars...

B) Islam is a religion of peace and love which has nothing to do with Merah and other murderers.

We would love nothing more than for this to be the case, to reassure millions of "unfaithfuls" in France and the rest of the world.

But how it is that the French Council of the Muslim Cult (CFCM), wishing to calm things and reassure, published what is really incendiary, *"Citizen Convention of Muslims for a way of Living Together",* as shown by Bernard Dick in article[7] published in the French site "Riposte Laïque"? Readers who can read French can find the entire story and its author's comments; however, let's review the Article 8 of this story, which reveals the ambiguities maintained by the same ones who should make their best for dissipating them and reassure us:

---

[7] http://ripostelaique.com/convention-citoyenne-des-musulmans-de-france-pour-le-vivre-ensemble-decoder-la-takiyya-du-cfcm.html

Article 8. While it wishes to celebrate the citizenship of Muslims, the CFCM finds as reference to "REFORM AND REVIVIFY" Islam in France, only Muslim authors of the 12th century (al-Ghazâli) and the 19th century (Al-Afghani and Abdo). But what is most shocking in the CFCM's approach is to follow the example of Rashid Rida, the inspirer and thinker of Hassan al-Banna who founded The Muslim Brotherhood in 1928. In 1898, Rida was the founder of the magazine AL-MANAR (The Lighthouse) for the promotion of universal Islam, advocating a return to the "right path," to the path followed by the pious ancestors (Al-Salaf Al-Saleh). He is the instigator of Salafism and follows in the most radical footsteps of the "scholars" of Islam, Ibn Taymiyya (1263-1328), Ibn Hanbal (780-855) and even Mohammad Ibn Abd Al-Wahab (1703-1792), the father of Wahhabism. It's good to know that Rashid Rida rejects any separation between spiritual and temporal and is the precentor of the caliphate: *"Islam is based on spiritual and temporal authorities [...], the Caliph is the head of the Muslims, the person responsible for their religious and temporal interests. Any government which leads out of obedience to the Sharia is on the wrong path of Islam. Boosting the separation of the government of the State and religion is saying the necessity of deleting the Muslim authority of the universe and eradicating the Sharia from the existence and submitting the Muslims to those who are not on the same religious path, those who are called the corrupt, the unjust, the non-believers. Because the Quran is the foundation of religion, it constantly rings into their ears [the Muslims] and calls them from the bottom of their heart in a perfect Arabic language: Those who do not govern by the laws of Allah are the non-believers. Those who do not govern by the laws of Allah are the unjust. Those who do not govern by the laws of Allah are the corrupt".*

The reference to Rashid Rida is astonishing: either the drafters of the convention ignore who Rashid Rida is, or they know him but use the name of a Muslim personality unknown in the West. In any case, by referring to Rashid Rida, the CFCM encourages Muslims to revolt against the secular state, its Constitution and its institutions. It is a factious behavior that falls under the law.

The conclusion of Bernard Dick, an attending gynecologist, born in a family of Eastern Christians and humanist if any is without appeal:

"After having largely reviewed this "Citizen Convention of Muslims of France for a way of Living Together", we think that it will not affect the Muslims. It is intended to denounce those who rightly link between jihad and Islam because this period is marked by the return of the jihadists [Muslims] returning from Syria and by the crime committed at the Jewish museum in Brussels, whose suspect, Mehdi Nemmouche, a Franco-Algerian Muslim with a chaotic history, indoctrinated at the prison stage and hardened by jihad in Syria, is in the same line of Crimes of Mohammad Merah: hatred of Jews, non-Muslims and the West. One must be blind or a coward not to recognize that the common denominator for these 21st century barbarians is Islam. The CFCM should leave its trickery there and show civic honesty. Politicians and the media will have to open their eyes, read this convention attentively, read between the lines and exculpate those who criticize Islam and who wish for this council the coup de grace of an enlightened head of state. Naïve are those who believe that Islam and democracy are compatible. The CFCM advocates living together but separately."

But how can we accept that in these times of jihad, of attacks, we accept on our soil discourses treating us as non-believers, unjust and corrupt when we know the extent of exactions that can be implemented by terrorists persuaded to accomplish the will of Allah?

An excellent article[8] about the "Hijrah" by our late friend Philippe Jallade appeared on the *Résistance Républicaine* (*Republican Resistance*) website and taught us something fundamental that clearly explains the issues and makes us understand why Muslims are so keen to assert their "Religion."

They have no choice, as is clearly seen in one of the many websites that guide Muslim believers based on the Quran and the Hadiths of Muhammad:

"To reside among non-Muslims one must comply with two conditions:

The first condition:

"The citizen must remain enclosed within his religion, so that he may access the necessary science, faith, and power to adhere firmly to a religion while also being wary of deviating from the true path. He must retain a singular attitude of aversion and dislike toward the non-believer [and toward disbelief in general]. He must not display friendship of affection toward them, for to consider them allies and friends contradicts the faith."

---

[8] http://resistancerepublicaine.eu/2014/le-retour-des-musulmans-en-pays-musulmans-est-une-obligation-pour-eux-la-hijrah-par-philippe-jallade/
9. http://www.3ilmchar3i.net/article-27037030.html

And he - Ta'ala - said: *"O you the believers! Do not take allies among Jews and Christians; they are allies one of the others.* Allah - Ta'ala said: *"You will not find, among the people who believe in Allah and in the last day, those who befriend those who oppose Allah and his messenger, even if they were their fathers, their sons, their brothers or the people of their tribe."* [3]

And those of you who take them for allies, become one of them. Allah does not guide the unjust. You will see, also, that those who have a sickness of the heart gravitate toward them and say, 'We fear that bad fortune may find us. But perhaps Allah will bring victory or an order from Him. Then they will regret their secret thoughts." [4]

The second condition: *"Let him be able to practice his religion openly, so that he can observe the rituals of Islam without prohibition. Do your prayers in groups if there are other people with whom to pray and to celebrate the Friday prayers; practice fasting, perform the Hadj [the pilgrimage] and other rituals of Islam. If one is not allowed these practices, then it is not permitted for him to remain [in this country], and it is required for him to emigrate [Hijrah] in this case."*

It's very clear. They do not have the choice. Either they manage to live in a Muslin way in a non-Muslim country, and refrain from forming friendships with non-believers or other non-Muslims, by imposing compulsory taxes on non-Muslims, ostensibly praying, fasting and other Quranic prescriptions... or they must go to a Muslim country.

We must read and re-read Philippe's article and this very clear Muslim site, to understand the consequences of what has happened in France since 1974 but especially since the creation of the CFCM (*French Council of the Muslim Cult*).

Muslims in France, [and in any other Western country] if they wish to apply the Quranic precepts, must impose their practices and prescriptions on non-Muslims. They cannot live like Christians, who practice discretely within the family circle and intimacy of their religion, the only pledge for living together and for freedom of religion, which guarantees secularism.

We perfectly understand what the late King of Morocco Hassan II meant when he said that Islam and secularism were incompatible in an interview granted to the French journalist Anne Sinclair in 1993

Things are clear. Either Occident is Islamized, or the "real" Muslims will have to leave it.

Conclusion

There is Muslim and Muslim, fortunately

In Islam, one does not choose one's religion, one does not have the right to leave it, it is enough to have a Muslim father to find oneself imprisoned in precepts dating back to the 7th century... Large numbers of "born Muslims" wish to live, for example, in France or in America without being forced to display their religion or practice it; they are for the most part atheists, agnostics, vaguely believers or simply of "Muslim culture." Most of them, moreover, have never read the Quran and cannot read or even speak Arabic.

Hence the concern caused by the creation of Koranic schools in growing numbers. The risk of indoctrinating children, vulnerable spirits in essence, and pushing them to apply literally what they read and learn is enormous. It would be absurd for us to give in any Western country the means to create jihadists and to make "born Muslims" terrorists!

It is up to us to fight so that they have this freedom that their co-religionists who closely follow the Islamic precepts refuse them... These are the "co-religionists" that we call "true" Muslims. Those who apply the Quranic precepts to the letter and are ready to kill to impose these precepts on all, non-Muslims and Muslims. If Muslims died in the attacks on the satirical magazine Charlie Hebdo in Paris (Jan 14, 2015) and on a Tunisian beach (June 26, 2015), it is because they worked for or sought to protect non-Muslims, Westerners, or Christians.

And it is these "true or devout Muslims" who slaughter, rape, kidnap, assassinate, cause explosions, forbid women the right to education and even health care, destroy the heritage of our civilization in Nineveh in a movement of refusal of everything which is not Islam. And hatred for everything that is not Islam.

That is why the distinction between Islam and Islamism is specious. According to Ferhat Mehenni, President of the Kabyle Provisional Government in exile in Paris, "*Islam is Islamism at rest and Islamism is Islam in motion. It's one and the same thing.*"

Islam is able to remain at rest when faced with strong powers that impose silence on Islamic law and make Islam a set of rites, essentially religious. This is what happened in Turkey with Atatürk, in Tunisia with Bourguiba, in French Algeria...

But when the Muslim parties are in power, they are capable of exerting pressure as we have seen during the "Arab Spring", or are constituted in Caliphate like the Islamic State, wherein the temptation to return to the source is very strong, and it allows the seduction of jihadist apprentices.

There can be no question for those who, Muslims or non-Muslims, live on Western soil, to let barbarism and terrorism prevail everywhere. It is therefore the duty of the rulers to take the necessary measures so that nowhere in the West can one read, repeat or teach hate verses encouraging young (and not so young) Muslims to take themselves for the Armed arm of Muhammad.

That is why a parliamentary committee should be appointed to shed light on the risks of terrorist training in our countries. It could also shed light on the compatibility between Islam, democracy, freedom of expression, freedom, equality and secularism, all the more so as some seek to impose its laws in the West by terrorism and Intimidation, inscribed in its sacred texts.

More than ever, we must ensure that the men and women who live on our territories do not die because of a medieval totalitarian system that would replace our system and our values.

Christine Tasin

PART 2

The Quran and the United States of America

by René D'Armor

Introduction: Quran, Hadiths, Sunnah...

The Quran is the sacred book of Islam, believed by Muslims to be the infallible word of God dictated to Muhammad through the medium of the angel Gabriel. Its implementation is the Islamic canonical law, the Sharia, based on the teachings of the Quran, the Hadiths (traditions of the Prophet Muhammad), and Sunnah (the orally transmitted record of the teachings, deeds and sayings of the Prophet Muhammad, as well as various reports about his companions), prescribing both religious and secular duties and sometimes retributive penalties for lawbreaking.

The Quran, the "Holy Book" of Islam, "religion of love, tolerance and peace" contains at least 109 verses that call Muslims to war with nonbelievers for the sake of Islamic rule (Source:http://www.thereligionofpeace.com/quran/023-violence.htm).

Some are quite graphic, with commands to chop off heads and fingers and kill infidels wherever they may be hiding. Muslims who do not join the fight are called "hypocrites" and warned that Allah will send them to Hell if they do not join the slaughter. ISIS (Islamic State in Iraq and Syria), also known as ISIL (Islamic State in Iraq and the Levant), or simply IS (Islamic State), or finally Da'ech (or Daech) are not "radicals" or "extremists" but simply devout Muslims rigorously applying the Quran.

Chapter 1

U.S. Constitution & Law versus Sharia Law

THE CONSTITUTION OF THE UNITED STATES OF AMERICA

"We the People of the United States, in Order to form a more perfect Union, establish Justice, insure domestic Tranquility, provide for the common Defense, promote the general Welfare, and secure the Blessings of Liberty to ourselves and our Posterity, do ordain and establish this Constitution for the United States of America."

The US Constitution is made of seven articles and twenty seven amendments which form the fundamentals of the American law

On November 19, 1863, Abraham Lincoln delivered the Gettysburg Address, which ends up as follows, " ...that this Nation, under God, shall have a new birth of freedom, and that government of the people, by the people, for the people, shall not perish from the earth ".

Per Sharia law, based on the principles found in the Quran and other Islamic religious and political texts:
- There is no freedom of religion;
- There is no freedom of speech;
- There is no freedom of thought;
- There is no freedom of artistic expression;
- There is no freedom of the press;
- There is no equality of peoples – a non-Muslim, a Kafir, is never equal to a Muslim;
- There is no equal protection under Sharia for different classes of people.

Justice is dualistic, with one set of laws for Muslim males and different laws for women and non-Muslims;
- There are no equal rights for women;
- Women can be beaten;
- A non-Muslim cannot bear arms;
- There is no democracy, since democracy means that a non-Muslim is equal to a Muslim;
- Our Constitution is a man-made document of ignorance that must submit to Sharia;
- Non-Muslims are third-class citizens;
- All governments must be ruled by Sharia law;
- Unlike common law, Sharia is not interpretative, nor can it be changed;
- There is no Golden Rule.

(From "*Sharia Law for Non-Muslims*" by Bill Warner)

1. Freedom of Religion

1st Amendment of the Constitution – *Freedom of religion, speech, and the press; rights of assembly and petition.*

"Congress shall make no law respecting an establishment of religion, or prohibiting the free exercise thereof; or abridging the freedom of speech, or of the press, or the right of the people peaceably to assemble, and to petition the Government for a redress of grievances."

Islamic Religion – "Religion" does not mean the same thing for Muslims as it does for most other religious adherents, that is: a section of life reserved for certain matters, and separate from other sections of life. This is not the Islamic world view; it never has been in the past, and modern attempts of making it so are seen as an aberration. Islam is a "total way of life." It provides guidance in every sphere of life, from individual cleanliness, rules of trade, to the structure and politics of the society. Islam can never be separated from social, political, or economic life. In other words, Islam is NOT just a religion; it is a complete civilization with a detailed political system, religion and a legal code, in one word: a "theocracy" governed by the Sharia.

Throughout history, being a Muslim has meant not only belonging to a religious community of fellow believers but also living under the Islamic Law (*). For Islamic Law is believed to be an extension of God's absolute sovereignty.

*(*)Living under the Islamic Law means living under the **Sharia**, or **sharia law**, which is the **Islamic** legal system derived from the religious precepts of **Islam**, particularly the Quran and the Hadiths.*

- From **Seyed Qutb**, Member of the Brotherhood, Egyptian writer, educator, and religious leader (1906-1966 [executed by hanging]), *"There is only one law which ought to be followed, and that is the Sharia."*

- From **Seyed Abul** A'ala Maududi, Indian-Pakistani scholar (1903-1979), *"Islam wishes to destroy all states and governments anywhere on the face of the earth which are opposed to the ideology and program of Islam regardless of the country or the nation which rules it. The purpose of Islam is to set up a State on the basis of its own ideology and program."*

Quran, Surat 47:19 – *"So know, [O Muhammad], that there is no deity except Allah and ask forgiveness for your sin and for the believing men and believing women. And Allah knows of your movement and your resting place."*

Quran, Surat 98:6 – *"Indeed, they who disbelieved among the People of the Scripture (*) and the polytheists will be* *in the fire of Hell, abiding eternally therein. Those are the worst of creatures."*

(*) *The **"People of the Scripture"** are the Jews and Christians.*

In Islam God is acknowledged the sole sovereign of human affairs, so there has never been a distinction between religious and state authority. In Christendom, the distinction between the two authorities are said to be based upon records in the New Testament of Jesus, asking his followers to render unto Caesar what was his and unto God what was His. Therefore throughout Christian history until the present times, there have always been two authorities: "God and Caesar", or "the Church and the State."

Quran, Surat 4:89 – *"They (the nonbelievers) wish you would disbelieve as they disbelieved so you would be alike. So do not take from among them allies until they emigrate for the cause of Allah. But if they turn away, then seize them and kill them wherever you find them and take not from among them any ally or helper." (*)*

(*) This is Jihad, "The Holy War" to convert the world to Islam.

Quran, Surat 4:76 (extract) – *"Those who believe fight in the cause of Allah..."*

2. Freedom of Speech

Sharia law is Islamic law, the basis for all demands that Muslims make on democratic societies. Sharia is a condensation and extrapolation of the Quran and the Sunnah.

Per the 1st amendment of the Constitution, Congress shall not abridge "the freedom of speech".

According to the Sharia, speech defaming Islam or Muhammad is considered "blasphemy" and is punishable by death or imprisonment.

Tafsir Al-Jalalayn (*) – Verse 33.57 – *"Indeed those who are injurious to God and His Messenger — and they are the disbelievers, who attribute to God what He is exalted above of such things as [His having] a son or a partner and they deny His Messenger — God has cursed them in this world and the Hereafter, He has banished them [from His mercy], and has prepared for them a humiliating chastisement, and that is the Fire."*

<u>Simply said</u>: Whoever makes a speech defaming Allah and His Messenger, the Prophet Muhammad (which includes portraits, caricatures, and all kinds of representations), is considered making a blasphemy and must be imprisoned or killed by fire.

(*) Tafsir Al-Jalalayn is a classical Sunni Tafsir (interpretation) composed in 1459 and completed in 1506.

3. Freedom of Thought

- **About becoming an apostate of Islam** - Sharia Law, that is the law system espoused and based upon Islamic beliefs, contradicts aspects of human rights. This is in no way more glaring than its restriction upon people from leaving Islam (*which is a condemnation to death***). While people should be free to practice their religion however they wish and agree to be governed as they desire in such matters, <u>denial of one's ability to leave is an affront to human rights</u>.

- Islam is NOT a religion as we, "nonbelievers", understand it, but rather a theocracy that hides behind the mask of religion to take over the entire world. Islam is the only so-called religion that has to retain its membership by threatening to kill anyone who leaves.

Bukhari* 9.84.57 (Persian Islamic Scolar – 810-870). *"The Prophet said, "Whoever changed his Islamic religion, then kill him."*

(Note: This Hadith has been confirmed by Dr. Sakir Naik, trained as a medical doctor before becoming a public speaker (born Oct. 1965 in Mumbai, India) who said, "If a Muslim changes his religion he should be killed.")

*Sahih al-Bukhari is a collection of **Hadiths** compiled by Imam **Muhammad al-Bukhari** (d. 256 AH/870 AD) (rahimahullah). His collection is recognized by the overwhelming majority of the Muslim world to be the most authentic collection of reports of the Sunnah of the Prophet Muhammad.)

**According to the historical context of Surat 5:33, which commands mutilation and crucifixion for striving against Allah and Muhammad, some Arab tribesmen turned away from Islam, but they also murdered a shepherd and stole livestock. Thus, more than apostasy is in view here. Nonetheless, the Hadith uses this context to justify death for apostates.

Quran, Surat 5:33 – *"Those who wage war against God and His Messenger and strive to spread corruption in the land should be punished by death, crucifixion, the amputation of an alternate hand and foot or banishment from the land: a disgrace* *for them in this world, and then a terrible punishment in the Hereafter...*" (MAS Abdel Haleem, The Quran, Oxford UP, 2004)

Bukhari 9,83,17 – Muhammad said: *"A Muslim who has admitted that there is no god but Allah and that I am His prophet may not be killed except for three reasons: as punishment for murder, for adultery, or for apostasy."*

- What about atheism? **Freedom of religion, and freedom from religion in America** –

http://atheism.about.com/od/churchstatemyths/a/freedomfrom.htm

This claim is common, but it rests on a misunderstanding of what real freedom of religion entails. The most important thing to remember is that freedom of religion, if it is going to apply to everyone, also requires freedom from religion. Why is that? You do not truly have the freedom to practice your religious beliefs if you are also required to adhere to any of the religious beliefs or rules of other religions.

What freedom from religion does mean, however, is the freedom from the rules and dogmas of other people's religious beliefs so that we can be free to follow the demands of our own conscience, whether they take a religious form or not.

Thus, we have both freedom of religion and freedom from religion because they are two sides of the same coin.

The Quran on disbelievers (including atheists):

Surat Al-'Anfāl (The Spoils of War) – Quran, Surat 8:7 (Sahih International) – *"[Remember, O believers], when Allah*

promised you one of the two groups (*) - that it would be yours - and you wished that the unarmed one would be yours. But Allah intended to establish the truth by His words and to eliminate the disbelievers."

(*) The two groups being *"believers"* and *"disbelievers"*

Quran, Surat 8:12-13: *"I (Allah) will cast terror into the hearts of those who disbelieved, so strike them upon the necks (*) and strike from them every fingertip. That is because they opposed Allah and His Messenger. And whoever opposes Allah and His Messenger – indeed, Allah is severe in penalty."*

(*) In plain English: "Behead them"

This verse orders Muslims to fight non-Muslims simply because they do not believe in the same God that Muslims do:

Quran, Surat 9:29 - Chapter (9) sūrat l-tawbah (The Repentance): *"Fight those who do not believe in Allah, nor in the latter day, nor do they prohibit what Allah and His Messenger have prohibited, nor follow the religion of truth, out of those who have been given the Book [Jews and Christians], until they pay the tax in acknowledgment of superiority and they are in a state of subjection."*

4. Freedom of Artistic Expression

Music, and some other forms of art (including tattooing), under Islamic law are forbidden. Western music and movies in particular, have been declared as corruptive influences by Islamic clerics. The vast majority of Islamic scholars and all four schools of Islamic jurisprudence are in agreement that listening to, or playing musical instruments, and singing is forbidden. They form this opinion from both the Quran and Hadith. The only exception to this rule which can be extracted from the Hadith is the permissibility of singing acapella accompanied by a duff (a hand-held one-sided drum) on special occasions (i.e. on weddings, Eid, during jihad etc.) This form of song is referred to as a **Nasheed**, and the striking of the duff is permitted for women only and must not be done in the presence of men.

Bukhari 7,72,843 – *"Muhammad grew depressed one day after Gabriel's promised visit was delayed. When Gabriel came at last, Muhammad complained about the delay. Gabriel said to him, "Angels will not enter a house that contains a dog or a picture."*

Those who make pictures will burn in Hell.

Bukhari 8,73,130 – *"There was once a curtain with pictures of animals on it in my house [Aisha's]. When Muhammad saw it, his face became flushed with anger. He tore it to bits and said, "People that paint such pictures will receive Hell's most terrible punishment on judgment Day."*

All literature must submit to the demands of Sharia. Muhammad repeatedly killed artists and intellectuals such as Kab, a poet, who wrote a poem criticizing Islam.

Quran, Surat 31:6 – *"And of the people is he who buys the amusement of speech [such as songs and music] to mislead [others] from the way of Allah without knowledge and who takes it in ridicule. Those will have a humiliating punishment."*

5. Freedom of the Press

Liberal democracy is committed to freedom of the press. Islam is not. Here is an editorial that was run in *USA Today* by a man identified as a teacher of Sharia law in Great Britain, January 24, 2015, (extract) "*Contrary to popular misconception, Islam does not mean peace but rather means submission to the commands of Allah alone. Therefore, Muslims do not believe in the concept of freedom of expression, as their speech and actions are determined by divine revelation and not based on people's desires.*"

These resources do not recognize individual freedom/rights, but rather the submission of all people to Islam (which means "submission")… willingly or under severe duress… to the will of the Muslim god Allah, as per the words of Muhammad.

6. No Equality of the People

In the Islamic system, there is no equality between a Muslim and a non-Muslim or a Kafir. Kafirs are more than non-believers. Kafirs are the "concealers": those who conceal the truth of Islam (i.e., Jews, Christians, Buddhists, Atheists, etc.)

The result of a control of Islam over democratic countries would be, at first, implementing in modern times the rules taken from a treaty with Christians in 637 AD, known as "The Treaty of Umar*". The rules are similar for Jews and others, in other words: the Kafirs.

***Umar** ibn Al-Khattāb, **Umar** Son of Al-Khattab, born 577 CE (Common Era. For example, Jesus was born in the fall some year between 7 and 4 BCE or Before CE) – died 3

November 644 CE), was one of the most powerful and influential Muslim caliphs (successors) in history. He was a senior Sahaba (companion) of the Islamic prophet Muhammad.

The Treaty of Umar

"We shall not build, in our cities or in their neighborhood new monasteries, churches, convents, or monks' cells, nor shall we repair, by day or by night, such of them as fallen in ruins or situated in the quarters of the Muslims."

"We shall keep our gates wide open for passersby and travelers. We shall give board and lodging to all Muslims who pass our way for three days."

"We shall not give shelter in our churches or in our dwellings to any spy nor hide him from the Muslims."

"We shall not manifest our religion publicly nor convert anyone to it. We shall not prevent any of our kin from entering Islam if they wish it."

"We shall show respect toward the Muslims, and we shall rise from our seats when they wish to sit."

"We shall not seek to resemble the Muslims by imitating any of their garments."

"We shall not mount on saddles, nor shall we gird swords nor bear any kind of arms not carry them on our persons."

"We shall not engrave Arabic inscriptions on our seals."

"We shall not sell fermented drinks (alcohol)."

"We shall clip the fronts of our heads (keep a short forelock as a sign of humiliation.)"

"We shall always dress in the same way wherever we may be, and we shall bind the zumar round our waists. (Christians and Jews had to wear special clothing.)"

"We shall not display our crosses or our books in the roads or markets of the Muslims. We shall only use clappers in our churches very softly. We shall not raise our voices when following our dead. We shall not take slaves who have been allotted to Muslims."

"We shall not build houses higher that the houses of the Muslims."

"Whoever strikes a Muslim with deliberate intent shall forfeit the protection of this pact."

(From Al-Turtushi, Siraj Al-Muluk, p. 229-30.)

7. No equal protection

a) – **Muslims versus non-Muslims** - Muslim propagandists use an attractive motto which says that Islam is the religion of justice and equality. It is the religion of freedom and women's dignity, they say, but this cannot be proved by mere talk and a loud voice.

Tell us where the justice and equality is in Islam when a Muslim's life is spared even if he kills a Christian intentionally while a Muslim may only be required to die if he assassinates another Muslim. The reason, as Muhammad said is that "*only Muslims' blood is regarded equal*." Thus, no Muslim should be killed for murdering a non-Muslim. If Muhammad says – according to all scholars – that "*only Muslims' blood is equal*" (have the same value), we have the right to ask, "Where, then, is equality?" Muhammad says to us, "*I meant the equality between a Muslim and another Muslim and not between a Muslim and a non-Muslim.*"

Unfortunately, there are very few verses of tolerance and peace to abrogate or even balance out the many that call for nonbelievers to be fought and subdued until they either accept humiliation, convert to Islam, or are killed. Muhammad's own martial legacy - and that of his companions - along with the remarkable stress on violence found in the Quran have produced a trail of blood and tears across world history.

Quran, Surat 3.56 – 'Āli `Imrān (Family of Imran) – *"And as for those who disbelieved, I will punish them with a severe punishment in this world and the Hereafter, and they will have no helpers."*

Quran, Surat 2:191-193 – *"And kill them wherever you find them, and turn them out from where they have turned you out. And Al-Fitnah [disbelief or unrest] is worse than killing... but if they desist, then lo! Allah is forgiving and merciful. And fight them until there is no more Fitnah [disbelief and worshipping of others along with Allah] and worship is for Allah alone. But if they cease, let there be no transgression except against Az-Zalimun (the polytheists, and wrong-doers, etc.)"*

(Translation is from the Noble Quran) The verse prior to this (190) refers to *"Fighting for the cause of Allah those who fight you",* leading some to believe that the entire passage refers to a defensive war in which Muslims are defending their homes and families. The historical context of this passage is not defensive warfare, however, since Muhammad and his Muslims had just relocated to Medina and were not under attack by their Meccan adversaries. In fact, the verses urge offensive warfare, in that Muslims are to drive Meccans out of their own city (which they later did). Verse 190 thus means to fight those who offer resistance to Allah's rule (i.e. Muslim conquest). The use of the word "persecution" by some Muslim translators is disingenuous (the actual Arabic words for persecution - "*idtihad*" - and oppression - a variation of "z-l-m" - do not appear in the verse). The word used instead, "*fitna*", can mean disbelief, or the disorder that results from unbelief or temptation. This is certainly what is meant in this context since the violence is explicitly commissioned *"until religion is for Allah"* – i.e. unbelievers desist in their unbelief.

Ibn Timiyya, born 1263, Harran, Mesopotamia—died September 26, 1328, Damascus, Syria, is one of Islam's most forceful theologians ; Ibn Timiyya emphasizes forcefully in Volume 14, p.85:

"Nothing in the law of Muhammad states that the blood of the disbeliever is equal to the blood of the Muslim because faith is necessary for equality. The people of the Covenant (Jews or Christians) do not believe in Muhammad and Islam, thus their blood and the Muslim's blood cannot be equal. These are distinctive texts which indicate that a Muslim is not to be put to death for (murdering) one of the people of the covenant or an

unbeliever, but a free Muslim must be killed for a free Muslim, regardless of the race."

b) - **Men and Women inequality** – Women are inferior to men in the Quran. For example:

1. Husbands are a degree above their wives in a legal context.

The Quran in Surat 2:228 says (extract): "... *Wives have the same rights as the husbands have on them in accordance with the generally known principles. Of course, men are a degree above them in status...*" (Sayyid Abul A'La Maududi, *the Meaning of the Quran*, vol. 1, p. 165)

2. A woman's testimony often counts half of a man's testimony.

The Quran in Surat 2:282 says (extract): "... *And let two men from among you bear witness to all such documents [contracts of loans without interest]. But if two men be not available, there should be one man and two women to bear witness so that if one of the women forgets (anything), the other may remind her.*" (Maududi, vol. 1, p. 205).

3. Men are superior to women in a domestic context.

The Quran in Surat 4:34 says (extract): *"... Men are managers of the affairs of women because Allah has made the one superior to the other."* (Maududi, vol. 1, p. 329)

8. No Equal Rights for Women

- **Status of Women in Islam** - One of the central concepts of Sharia Law is that women are to be treated as second class citizens. This violates so many aspects of human rights as declared by the United Nations in 1948 that there isn't sufficient space here to list them all.

- **Inheritance** - According to the Quran (Surat An-Nisā' [The Women]), a woman inherits half of what a man inherits.

Quran, Surat 4:11 – *"Allah instructs you concerning your children: for the male, what is equal to the share of two females. But if there are [only] daughters, two or more, for them is two thirds of one's estate. And if there is only one, for her is half. And for one's parents, to each one of them is a sixth of his estate if he left children. But if he had no children and the parents [alone] inherit from him, then for his mother is one third. And if he had brothers [or sisters], for his mother is a sixth, after any bequest he [may have] made or debt. Your parents or your children - you know not which of them are nearest to you in benefit. [These shares are] an obligation [imposed] by Allah. Indeed, Allah is ever Knowing and Wise."*

Note: Plain English translation: one man is worth two women!

- **Female Genital Mutilation, or Female Circumcision** - Bukhari 7,72,779 – *"Muhammad said, "Five practices are characteristics of ancient prophets: circumcision, shaving the pubic hair, cutting the moustaches short, clipping the nails, and depilating the hair of the armpits."*

Note- This Hadith refers to the circumcision of both the removal of the foreskin of the male and the removal of the clitoris

(Hufaad) of the woman, although there is no comparison. Circumcision is part of the Sharia law.

Female Genital Mutilation (FGM) damages the sex organs, inhibiting pleasure and causing severe pain and complications for women's sexual and reproductive health. The Population Reference Bureau conducted a nationwide prevalence study on FGM, released in February 2015 that estimates up to 507,000 women and girls living in the U.S. are at risk of or have undergone FGM, partly because of an influx of immigrants from the 29 countries where FGM is practiced.

The federal law addresses FGM in the U.S. is **18 U.S. Code § 116 'Female Genital Mutilation'**. The law makes it illegal to perform FGM in the U.S. or knowingly transport a girl out of the U.S. for purpose of inflicting FGM.

18 U.S. Code § 116(d) states: *"Whoever knowingly transports from the United States and its territories a person in foreign commerce for the purpose of [female genital mutilation] with regard to that person that would be a violation of subsection (a) if the conduct occurred within the United States, or attempts to do so, shall be fined under this title or imprisoned not more than 5 years, or both."*

Note: Although there is no reference to it in the Quran, FGM is found mostly within and adjacent to Muslim communities in Central-North Africa, but it is not required by Islam or practiced in most Muslim countries, and prevalence rates vary according to ethnicity, not religion.

Among social activists and feminists, combating female genital mutilation (FGM) is an important policy goal. Sometimes called female circumcision or female genital cutting,

FGM is the cutting of the clitoris of girls in order to curb their sexual desire and preserve their sexual honor before marriage. The practice, prevalent in some majority Muslim countries, has a tremendous cost: many girls bleed to death or die of infection. Most are traumatized. Those who survive can suffer adverse health effects during marriage and pregnancy. New information from Iraqi Kurdistan raises the possibility that the problem is more prevalent in the Middle East than previously believed and that FGM is far more tied to religion than many Western academics and activists admit.

http://www.meforum.org/1629/is-female-genital-mutilation-an-islamic-problem

What is needed is a ZERO TOLERANCE against this disgusting and barbaric practice.

- <u>Polygamy</u> - Polygamy is defined as the practice or condition of having more than one spouse at the same time, conventionally referring to a situation where all spouses know about each other, in contrast to bigamy, where two or more spouses are usually unaware of each other.

Polygamy and bigamy are illegal in the United States (*). The crime is punishable by a fine, imprisonment, or both, according to the law of the individual state and the circumstances of the offense.

(*) <u>Note</u>: Still, Muslims practice polygamy in the U.S., despite state laws prohibiting it. Here's how a man gets around the laws: He marries one woman under civil law, and then marries one, two or three others in religious ceremonies that are not recognized by the state. In other cases, men marry women in both

America and abroad. Many women keep quiet for fear of retribution or deportation.

Quran, Surat 4:3 – *"If ye fear that ye shall not be able to deal justly with the orphans, Marry women of your choice, two or three or four; but if ye fear that ye shall not be able to deal justly (with them), then only one, or (a captive) that your right hands possess, that will be more suitable, to prevent you from doing injustice."*

- Pedophilia and/or Child Sexual Abuse – This highly controversial Quranic verse prescribes the waiting period of a female who has not yet reached puberty thereby permitting men to have sex with girls who have not reached puberty. Under federal law, offenders convicted of sexually abusing a child face fines and imprisonment. Furthermore, an offender may face harsher penalties if the crime occurred in aggravated circumstances, which include, for example, the offender used force or threats, inflicted serious bodily injury or death, or kidnapped a child in the process of committing child sexual abuse.

Marrying a young girl before she reaches the age of adolescence is permitted in Sharia; indeed it was narrated that there was scholarly consensus on this point. It is historically known that the Prophet married 'Aa'ishah when she was six years old and consummated the marriage when she was nine.

Al-Nawawi (1233–1277), popularly known as al-Nawawi, an-Nawawi or Imam Nawawi (631–676 A.H./1234–1277), was a Sunni Muslim author on Fiqh *[islamic jurisprudence]* and Hadith; he said: *"With regard to the wedding-party of a young married girl at the time of consummating the marriage, if the husband and the guardian of* *the girl agree upon something that will not cause harm to the young girl, then that may be done"*. If they disagree, then Ahmad, who claimed that he was the awaited Messiah (1889), and Abu 'Ubayd (Persian Physician, 1014-1094) said that when a girl reaches the age of nine then the marriage may be consummated even without her consent. *(In civilized language, this is "rape".)*

Quran, Surat 65:4 – *"Such of your women as have passed the age of monthly courses, for them the prescribed period, if you have any doubts (about their periods), is three months, and for those who have no courses (i.e. they are still immature), their "iddah" (prescribed period) is three months likewise."*

- Sex with women who are prisoners of war – The Quran (Surat 33:50) literally means that Muhammad LEGALIZED sex with slave girls/women that they captured in their raids. Muhammad gave himself permission to have sex with anyone he wanted to. Notice the phrases "*this only for thee*" and "*in order that there should be no difficulty for thee.*" Everyone who has ever read the Quran & Hadiths know that he gave captured girls to his male followers to have sex with & permission to brutalize them in other ways.

Quran, Surat 33:50 – *"O Prophet! We have made lawful to thee the wives to whom thou hast paid their dowers, and those whom thy right hand possesses out of the prisoners of war whom Allah has assigned to thee; and daughters of thy paternal uncles and aunts, and daughters of thy maternal uncles and aunts, who migrated (from Makka) with thee; and any believing woman who dedicates her soul to the Prophet if the Prophet wishes to wed her, this is only for thee, and not for the Believers [at large]). We know what We have appointed for them as to their wives and the captives whom their right hands* *possess, in order that there should be no difficulty for thee. And Allah is Oft-Forgiving, MostMerciful."*

9. Women Can Be Beaten

Women aren't allowed to do much of anything other than wear a veil and do what their husbands tell them to do, and the punishments for violating these rules are incredibly severe.

From **Muhammad Ibn Ishaq**, Arab Muslim historian (704-768) – *"Men were to lay injunctions on women lightly, for they were prisoners of men and had no control over their persons."*

Quran, Surat 4:34 - Sahih International – *"Men are in charge of women by [right of] what Allah has given one over the other and what they spend [for maintenance] from their wealth. So righteous women are devoutly obedient, guarding in [the husband's] absence what Allah would have them guard. But those [wives] from whom you fear arrogance - [first] advise them; [then if they persist], forsake them in bed; and [finally], strike them. But if they obey you [once more], seek no means against them. Indeed, Allah is ever Exalted and Grand.*

Note: In short, this verse advises men to beat their wives if they don't obey them.

10. A non-Muslim Cannot Bear Arms

Second Amendment of the Constitution: ***Right to bear arms:*** *"A well-regulated Militia, being necessary to the security of a Free State, the right of the people to keep and bear Arms, shall not be infringed."*

Sharia: Under historic and modern laws about *dhimmi (nonbelievers)*, non-Muslims cannot possess swords, firearms or weapons of any kind. Freedom of the press is related to the right to keep and bear arms.

From the **Treaty of Umar** (see above) – *"We shall not mount on saddles, nor shall we gird swords nor bear any kind of arms not carry them on our persons."*

11. There is No Democracy in Islam

Islam is the opposite of democracy - Any human law can be amended. Quran and its law, Sharia, come from the only legitimate god, Allah, and as such is NOT interpretative and cannot be amended. So in short legislation of Allah and legislation of people cannot be equal.

Quran, Surat 6:57 – *"Allah is the only law-maker, legislator. Allah has given us laws which we have to implement as His subordinate on our personal lives and on state and in our homes as well."*

Islamic law and Democracy are incompatible. Moroccan-born **Hamza Chaoui**, a controversial Montreal Imam has described Islam and democracy as "completely" incompatible.

During an interview published on September 14, 2015, **Grand Ayatollah Ahmad al-Baghdadi**, the leading Shia cleric of Iraq made clear why Islam and the rest of the world can never peacefully coexist. According to the ayatollah, when they can— when circumstance permits it, when they are strong enough— Muslims are obligated to go on the offensive and conquer non-Muslims (a fact to be kept in mind as millions of Muslim "refugees" flood the West).

Following is an extract of the interview, *"If they are people of the book [Jews and Christians] we demand of them the jizya (tax), and if they refuse, then we fight them. That is if he is*

Christian, he has three choices: either convert to Islam, or, if he refuses and wishes to remain Christian, then pay the jizya [and live according to dhimmi rules]. But if they still refuse, then we fight them, and we abduct their women, and destroy their churches. This is Islam!"

http://www.jihadwatch.org/2015/10/raymond-ibrahim-abducting-women-and-destroying-churches-is-real-islam-says-iraqi-grand-ayatollah

12. Our Constitution is a Man-made Document of Ignorance

"ISLAMIC SCHOLARS CLAIM: Islamic law is perfect, universal and eternal. The laws of the United States are temporary, limited and will pass away. It is the duty of every Muslim to obey the laws of Allah, the Sharia. US laws are man-made; while Sharia law is sacred and comes from the only legitimate god, Allah."
(*"Sharia Law for Non-Muslims"* by Bill Warner)

13. Non-Muslims are Third-class Citizens

How many Islamic countries offer non-Muslims the same civil rights as their Muslim citizens? According to Islam, Muslims are first-class citizens. Jews and Christians are second-class citizens. Anybody else is third-class citizen, or "dhimmis". Of course everybody must obey the Islamic law.

"In an Islamic State, Islam is the ideology of the State and, therefore, there is no room for those who are outside the State's ideology in the government, they are seen as third-class citizens or aliens and possibly, dangerous creatures whose loyalty is questioned and always suspect."

(From "Islamic Jerusalem and its Christians" by Maher Y. Abu-Munshar)

14. All Governments must be ruled by Sharia law

"Islam shares many similarities with Nazism. Both movements had a burning, irrational, unquenchable hatred of the Jews. Both movements have a theory of the Master Race. In the case of Islam, Muslims are considered the very best of people. While non-Muslims are the equivalent of the "Untermenschen" or sub humans. Non-Muslims are considered to be filth. In polite circles, the word filth means excrement. ***All of us who are non-Muslims can be killed with impunity by Muslims. It is not even considered a crime under Sharia Law.***" **(John Constantine)**

http://sheikyermami.com/2014/06/tabari-969-killing-unbelievers-is-a-small-matter-to-us-2/)

Quran, Surat 47:4 - *Muhammad said, "You are commanded to carry out jihad against the unbelieving infidels until they submit to Islam".*

Quran, Surat 8:39 – *"And fight with them until there is no more persecution and religion should be only for Allah."*

Al-Tabari 9:69 (Persian Scholar, 838-923) – *"Killing Unbelievers is a small matter to us."*

Simply stated, all "infidels" have to submit to Islam, to the Sharia law, or be killed…

15. Sharia is not interpretative

Any human law can be amended. The US Constitution contains twenty seven amendments, and more might come in the future as the world changes. The Islamic way of life is 1400 years old, as dictated by Allah to Muhammad and as such is NOT interpretative and cannot be amended. So in short legislation of Allah and legislation of the people, by the people, for the people cannot be equal.

Quran, Surat 6:57 – *"Allah is the only law-maker, legislator. Allah has given us laws which we have to implement as His subordinate on our personal lives and on state and in our homes as well."*

Moreover, we must stop seeing Islam as a religion only, it's a complete socio-economic political system. Hence, how can Islam be accepted in a democratic country under the freedom of religion while Quran and Sharia are taught in mosques?

Quran, Surat 5 44 – *"And whoever does not judge by what Allah has revealed, then they are the disbelievers."*

Quran, Surat 5 45 – *"And whoever does not judge by what Allah has revealed - then it is those who are the wrongdoers."*

Quran, Surat 5 47 – *"And whoever does not judge by what Allah has revealed - then it is those who are the defiantly disobedient."*

16. There is no Golden Rule

The **Golden Rule** or **ethic of reciprocity** is a maxim, ethical code or morality that essentially states either of the following:

• One should treat others as one would like to treat oneself (directive form)

• One should not treat others in ways one would not like to be treated (cautionary form, also known as the Silver Rule.

This concept describes a "reciprocal", or "two-way", relationship between one's self and others that involves both sides equally, and in a mutual fashion. *(Wikipedia)*

The problem with the good teachings of Muhammad is that they are reserved for fellow Muslims. When the Hadith says *"None of you [truly] believes until he wishes for his brother what he wishes for himself.,."* it is talking about the fellow Muslims. The brotherhood in Islam does not extend to everyone. The **Quran (9:23)** states that the believers should not take for friends and protectors (awlia) their fathers and brothers if they love Infidelity above Islam. In fact there are many verses that tell the Muslims to kill the unbelievers and be harsh to them. A clear example that Islam is not based on the Golden Rule is the verse (48:29): *"Muhammad is the messenger of Allah; and those who are with him are strong against Unbelievers, (but) compassionate amongst each other."* This is the perfect definition of fascism.

(Source: http://www.jihadwatch.org/2009/05/islam-and-the-golden-rule)

Note: Those principles of the Sharia law, far from being exhaustive, are in absolute contradiction with the US Constitution and the American law, and should be enough to declare the Quran *(taught in mosques)* illegal in the United States of America... And there is more!

Islamic law and American law

WASHINGTON, May 19, 2015 (UPI) -- Does Islamic law, Sharia, have a place in American courts? A lot of state legislatures don't think so, and there is a movement to ban its application in domestic courts, state and federal.

It's one of those national issues that for now is not before the U.S. Supreme Court, but almost inevitably will be before the justices somewhere down the line, even if just in the petition stage.

Sharia, based on the sayings of the Prophet Muhammad, is often a consideration in family issue cases involving U.S. Muslims. But its precepts apply to all aspects of life, and its severest critics allege it is a factor in some acts of terror, because Islam is a total system of life: it's all together a social system, a judicial system, a political system which includes geo-political aspirations.

How widespread is the movement to ban Sharia and any foreign law from domestic courts?

In 2014 Alabama became the eighth state to ban Sharia law, voters overwhelmingly passed the Amendment to the State Constitution passed by a margin of 72 to 28, Alabama joined Arizona, Kansas, Louisiana, North Carolina, Oklahoma,

South Dakota, and Tennessee which also have bans on Sharia law, all but 16 states have considered such a law in the past 5 years.

Poll among American Muslims. June 24, 2015. (Source: http://www.breitbart.com/national-security/2015/06/24/shock-poll-51-of-american-muslims-want-sharia-25-okay-with-violence-against-americans/)

- **The Center for Security Policy** released a poll that should give all Americans pause! The results show that a startling number of American Muslims, our fellow citizens, agree that violence is a legitimate response to those who insult Islam. A full majority of 51% agreed that *"Muslims in America should have the choice of being governed according to Sharia."*

- Even more troubling, is the fact that nearly a quarter of the Muslims polled believed that, *"It is legitimate to use violence to punish those who give offense to Islam by, for example, portraying the prophet Mohammed."*

- In other words, a full 25% of those polled agreed that *"violence against Americans here in the United States can be justified as part of the global jihad."*

For those who don't know, Sharia Law is nothing less than the Nazification of a religion. Sharia authorizes murder against non-believers who won't convert, horrific oppression of women, the execution of gays, the extermination of Jews, and the beheading of anyone who draws Muhammad.

"Since Sharia is based on the Quran and the Sunnah of Muhammad, it is inevitable that Sharia would contain the same fundamental principles. The first principle of Islam is that the entire world must submit to Allah and follow the Sunnah of Muhammad. Sharia demands that our institutions submit to Islam:

- Our schools must submit in how they teach about Islam;

- Our media must present Islam in a good light."

("Sharia Law for Non-Muslims" by Bill Warmer*)*

Article 6 of the US Constitution states that *"This Constitution, and the Laws of the United States which shall be made in Pursuance thereof; and all Treaties made, or which shall be made, under the Authority of the United States, shall be the supreme Law of the Land; and the Judges in every State shall be bound thereby, any Thing in the Constitution or Laws of any State to the Contrary notwithstanding."*

The fundamental claim of Sharia is that it is the highest law in the world and that all other legal codes must submit to Islamic law. There is a massive contradiction that is being ignored as Sharia law is being implemented under the guise of Freedom of Religion. (*"Sharia Law for Non-Muslims"* by Bill Warner)

Chapter 2

The Quran, a Manual of Hate & War

The Mujahideen

Quran, Surat 4:95 – *"Not equal are those believers remaining [at home] - other than the disabled - and the mujahideen, [who strive and fight] in the cause of Allah with their wealth and their lives. Allah has preferred the mujahideen through their wealth and their lives over those who remain [behind], by degrees. And to both Allah has promised the best [reward: Paradise]. But Allah has preferred the mujahideen over those who remain [behind] with a great reward."*

This passage criticizes "peaceful" Muslims who do not join in the violence, letting them know that they are less worthy in Allah's eyes. It also demolishes the modern myth that "Jihad" doesn't mean holy war in the Quran, but rather a spiritual struggle. Not only is this Arabic word (mujahideen) used in this passage, but it is clearly not referring to anything spiritual, since the physically disabled are given exemption. (The Hadith reveals the context of the passage to be in response to a blind man's protest that he is unable to engage in Jihad, which would not make sense if it meant an internal struggle). According to the verse, Allah will allow the disabled into Paradise, but will provide a larger reward to those who are able to kill others in his cause.

Quran, Surat 2:116 – *"Fighting has been enjoined upon you while it is hateful to you. But perhaps you hate a thing and it is good for you; and perhaps you love a thing and it is bad for you. And Allah knows, while you know not."*

Not only does this verse establish that violence can be virtuous, but it also contradicts the myth that fighting is intended only in self-defense, since the audience was obviously not under attack at the time. From the Hadith, we know that this verse was narrated at a time that Muhammad was actually trying to motivate his people into raiding merchant caravans for loot.

Quran, Surat 3:151 – *"We will cast terror into the hearts of those who disbelieve for what they have associated with Allah of which He had not sent down [any] authority. And their refuge will be the Fire, and wretched is the residence of the wrongdoers."*

This speaks directly of polytheists, yet it also includes Christians, since they believe in the Trinity (i.e. what Muhammad incorrectly believed to be 'joining companions to Allah').

Quran, Surat 4:74 – *"So let those fight in the cause of Allah who sell the life of this world for the Hereafter. And he who fights in the cause of Allah and is killed or achieves victory - We will bestow upon him a great reward."*

The martyrs of Islam are unlike the early Christians, who were led meekly to the slaughter. These Muslims are killed in battle as they attempt to inflict death and destruction for the cause of Allah. This is the theological basis for today's suicide bombers.

Quran, Surat 4:104 – *"And do not weaken in pursuit of the enemy. If you should be suffering - so are they suffering as you are suffering..."*

Quran, Surat 5:33 – *"Indeed, the penalty for those who wage war against Allah and His Messenger and strive upon earth [to cause] corruption is none but that they be killed or crucified or that their hands and feet be cut off from opposite sides or that they be exiled from the land. That is for them a disgrace in this world; and for them in the Hereafter is a great punishment."*

Quran, Surat 8:12 – *"[Remember] when your Lord inspired to the angels, "I am with you, so strengthen those who have believed. I will cast terror into the hearts of those who disbelieved, so strike [them] upon the necks and strike from them every fingertip."*

No reasonable person would interpret these verses to mean a spiritual struggle.

Quran, Surat 8:15 – *"O you who have believed, when you meet those who disbelieve advancing [for battle], do not turn your backs to them."*

Quran, Surat 8:16 – *"And whoever turns his back to them on such a day, unless swerving [as a strategy] for war or joining [another] company, has certainly returned with anger [upon him] from Allah, and his refuge is Hell - and wretched is the destination."*

Quran, Surat 8:39 – *"And fight them until there is no fitnah and [until] the religion, all of it, is for Allah. And if they cease - then indeed, Allah is seeing of what they do."*

Note: Some translations interpret "fitnah" as "persecution", but the traditional understanding of this word is not supported by the historical context. The Meccans were simply refusing Muhammad access to their city during Haj. Other Muslims were allowed to travel there - just not as an armed group, since Muhammad had declared war on Mecca prior to his eviction. The Meccans were also acting in defense of their religion, since it was Muhammad's intention to destroy their idols and establish

Islam by force (which he later did). Hence the critical part of this verse is to fight until "religion is only for Allah", meaning that the true justification of violence was the unbelief of the opposition. According to the Sira (Ibn Ishaq/Hisham 324) Muhammad further explains that "Allah must have no rivals."

Quran, Surat 9:29 – *"Fight those who do not believe in Allah or in the Last Day and who do not consider unlawful what Allah and His Messenger have made unlawful and who do not adopt the religion of truth from those who were given the Scripture (the People of the Book) - [fight] until they pay the Jizya with willing submission and feel themselves subdued."*

"People of the Book" refers to Christians and Jews. According to this verse, they are to be violently subjugated, with the sole justification being their religious status. Verse 9:33 tells Muslims that Allah has charted them to make Islam "superior over all religions." This chapter was one of the final "revelations" from Allah and it set in motion the tenacious military expansion, in which Muhammad's companions managed to conquer two-thirds of the Christian world in the next 100 years. Islam is intended to dominate all other people and faiths.

Quran, Surat 9:73 – *"O Prophet! Strive hard against the unbelievers and the hypocrites and be unyielding to them; and their abode is hell, and evil is the destination."*

Quran, Surat 9:88 – *"But the Messenger, and those who believe with him, strive and fight with their wealth and their persons: for them are (all) good things: and it is they who will prosper."*

Dehumanizing those who reject Islam, by reminding Muslims that unbelievers are merely firewood for Hell, makes it easier to justify slaughter. It also explains why today's devout Muslims have little regard for those outside the faith.

Quran, Surat 9:123 – *"O you who have believed, fight those adjacent to you of the disbelievers and let them find in you harshness. And know that Allah is with the righteous."*

Quran, Surat 17:16 – *"And when We intend to destroy a city, We command its affluent but they defiantly transgress therein; so the word comes into effect upon it, and We destroy it with utter destruction."*

Note that the crime is moral transgression, and the punishment is "utter destruction." (Before ordering the 9/11 attacks, Osama bin Laden first issued Americans an invitation to Islam).

Quran, Surat 9:111 – *"Indeed, Allah has purchased from the believers their lives and their properties [in exchange] for that they will have Paradise. They fight in the cause of Allah, so they kill and are killed. [It is] a true promise [binding] upon Him in the Torah and the Gospel and the Quran. And who is truer to his covenant than Allah? So rejoice in your transaction which you have contracted. And it is that which is the great attainment."*

This is how the Quran defines true believers, *"They fight in the cause of Allah, so they kill and are killed."*

Quran, Surat 25:52 – *"Therefore listen not to the Unbelievers, but strive against them with the utmost strenuousness."*

"Strive against" is Jihad - obviously not in the personal context. It's also significant to point out that this is a Meccan verse.

Quran, Surat 33:60-62 – *"If the hypocrites, and those in whose hearts is a disease, and the alarmists in the city do not cease, We verily shall urge thee on against them, then they will be your neighbors in it but a little while. Accursed, they will be seized wherever found and slain with a (fierce) slaughter."*

This passage sanctions the slaughter against three groups:

- Hypocrites (Muslims who refuse to "fight in the way of Allah" (3:167) and hence don't act as Muslims should);

- Those with "diseased hearts" (which include Jews and Christians 5:51-52); and

- "Alarmists" or "Agitators" who include those who merely speak out against Islam, according to Muhammad's biographers.

Quran, Surat 47:3-4 – *"Those who disbelieve follow falsehood, while those who believe follow the truth from their Lord... So, when you meet (in fight Jihad in Allah's Cause), those who disbelieve smite at their necks till when you have killed and wounded many of them, then bind a bond firmly (*on them, i.e. take them as captives) .. *If it had been Allah's Will, He Himself could certainly have punished them (without you). But (He lets you fight), in order to test you, some with others. But those who are killed in the Way of Allah, He will never let their deeds be lost."*

Those who reject Allah are to be killed in Jihad. The wounded are to be held captive for ransom. The only reason Allah doesn't do the dirty work himself is to test the faithfulness of Muslims. Those who kill pass the test.

Quran, Surat 48:17 – *"There is not upon the blind any guilt or upon the lame any guilt or upon the ill any guilt* [for remaining behind]. *And whoever obeys Allah and His Messenger - He will admit him to gardens beneath which rivers flow; but whoever turns away - He will punish him with a painful punishment."*

The blind, lame and sick are excused. All other Muslims must fight to go to Paradise. This verse also says that those who do not fight will suffer torment in hell.

Quran, Surat 61:4 – *"Indeed, Allah loves those who fight in His cause in a row as though they are a [single] structure joined firmly."*

Religion of Peace, indeed! The verse explicitly refers to physical conflict. This is followed by 61:9 (see below).

Quran, Surat 61:9 – *"He it is who has sent His Messenger (Muhammad) with guidance and the religion of truth (Islam) to make it victorious over all religions even though the infidels may resist."*

Infidels who resist Islamic rule are to be fought (See next verse below).

Quran, Surat 66:9 – *"O Prophet! Strive against the disbelievers and the hypocrites, and be stern with them. Hell will be their home, a hapless journey's end."*

This is "Jihad", the context is clearly holy war, and the scope of violence is broadened to include "hypocrites" - those who call themselves Muslims but do not act as such.

Parts of Bukhari Hadith compilations (a call to war against the Jews and pagans)

From the Hadiths by Bukhari - Abū 'Abd Allāh Muḥammad ibn Ismā'īl ibn Ibrāhīm ibn al-Mughīrah ibn Bardizbah al-Ju'fī al-Bukhārī (19 July 810 – September 870), or Bukhārī, commonly referred to as Iman al-Bukhari or Iman Bukhari, was a Persian Islamic scholar who authored the Hadiths collection known as *Sahib al-Bukhari,* regarded by Sunni Muslims as one of the most *sahih* (authentic) of all *hadith* compilations.

- **Bukhari (52:177)** – *"Allah's Apostle said, "The Hour will not be established until you fight with the Jews, and the stone* *behind which a Jew will be hiding will say. "O Muslim! There is a Jew hiding behind me, so kill him."*

- **Bukhari (52:256)** – *"The Prophet... was asked whether it was permissible to attack the pagan warriors at night with the probability of exposing their women and children to danger. The Prophet replied, "They (*i.e. women and children*) are from them (*i.e. pagans*)."*

- **Bukhari (52:65)** – *"The Prophet said, "He who fights that Allah's Word, Islam, should be superior, fights in Allah's Cause."*

- **Bukhari (52:220)** – *"Allah's Apostle said... "I have been made victorious with terror."*

- **Bukhari (8:387)** – *"Allah's Apostle said, "I have been ordered to fight the people till they say: 'None has the right to be worshipped but Allah'. And if they say so, pray like our prayers, face our Qibla (*direction of Mecca*) and slaughter as we slaughter, then their blood and property will be sacred to us and we will not interfere with them except legally."*

- **Bukhari (52:73)** - *"Allah's Apostle said, 'Know that Paradise is under the shades of swords'."*

- **Bukhari (11:626)** - *[Muhammad said:] "I decided to order a man to lead the prayer and then take a flame to burn all those, who had not left their houses for the prayer, burning them alive inside their homes "*

- **Bukhari (1:35)** - *"The person who participates in (Holy Battles) in Allah's cause and nothing compels him do so except belief in Allah and His Apostle, will be recompensed by Allah either with a reward, or booty (if he survives) or will be admitted to Paradise (if he is killed)."*

Other than the fact that Muslims haven't killed every non-Muslim under their domain, there is very little else that they can point to as proof that theirs is a peaceful, tolerant religion. Where Islam is dominant (as in the Middle East and Pakistan), religious minorities suffer brutal persecution with little resistance. Where Islam is in the minority (as in Thailand, the Philippines and Europe), there is the threat of violence if Muslim demands are not met. Either situation seems to provide a justification for religious terrorism, which is persistent and endemic to Islamic fundamentalism.

Far from being mere history or theological construct, the violent verses of the Quran have played a key role in very real massacre and genocide. This includes the brutal slaughter of tens of millions of Hindus for five centuries beginning around 1000 AD with Mahmud of Ghazni's bloody conquest. Both he and the later Tamerlane (Islam's Genghis Khan) slaughtered an untold number merely for defending their temples from destruction.

Buddhism was very nearly wiped off the Indian subcontinent. Judaism and Christianity met the same fate (albeit more slowly) in areas conquered by Muslim armies, including the Middle East, North Africa and parts of Europe, including today's Turkey. Zoroastrianism, the ancient religion of a proud Persian people is despised by Muslims and barely survives in modern Iran.

So ingrained is violence in the religion that Islam has never really stopped being at war, either with other religions or with itself.

Dr. Salah al-Sawy, the chief member of the Assembly of Muslim Jurists in America, previously Professor in the Faculty of Legislation and Law at Al-Azhar, Cairo, stated in 2009 that "*The Islamic community does not possess the strength to engage in offensive jihad at this time*," tacitly affirming the legitimacy of violence for the cause of Islamic rule - bound only by the capacity for success.

Chapter 3

Jihad

From *"American Sniper"* by Chris Kyle, page 86, *"The people we were fighting in Iraq, after Saddam's army fled or was defeated, were fanatics. They hated us because we weren't Muslims. They wanted to kill us, even though we'd just booted out their dictator, because we practiced a different religion than they did. Isn't religion supposed to teach tolerance?"*

"Because They Hate", such is the title of a book written by Brigitte Gabriel, American journalist, author, social commentator, and activist, originally from a Christian family in Lebanon. That's the answer given to her by her father when she was a young girl and asked him why the Muslims were killing them. *"Because they hate"* was her dad's answer.

Mawlana Abul Ala Mawdudi, and Indian-Pakistani scholar, philosopher, jurist, journalist, islamist and Iman, said, *"Islam is not a normal religion like the other religions in the world, and Muslim nations are not like normal nations. Muslim nations are very special because they have a command from Allah to rule the entire world and to be over every nation in the world."*

Quran, Surat 2:257 – *"Allah is the ally of those who believe. He brings them out from darkness into the light. And those who disbelieve - their allies are Taghut (*off limits… People who overstep boundaries*). They take them out of the light into darkness. Those are the companions of the Fire; they will abide eternally therein. (They will be sent to Hell where they will stay forever)."*

Quran, Surat 5:105 – *"O you who believe! Take care of your own selves. If you follow the (right) guidance [and enjoin what is right (*Islamic Monotheism and all that Islam orders one to do*) and forbid what is wrong (*polytheism, disbelief and all that Islam has forbidden*)], no hurt can come to you from those who are in error."*

From the Islamic Supreme Council of America: (http://islamicsupremecouncil.org/understanding-islam/legal-rulings/5-jihad-a-misunderstood-concept-from-islam.html?start=9),

"The Arabic word 'jihad' is often translated as 'holy war', but in a purely linguistic sense, the word 'jihad' means struggling or striving. The Arabic word for war is 'al-harb.' – Jihad is not a violent concept. Jihad is not a declaration of war against other religions. It is worth noting that the Quran specifically refers to Jews and Christians as 'people of the book' who should be protected and respected. All three faiths worship the same God. Allah is just the Arabic word for God, and is used by Christian Arabs as well as Muslims."

This quote is nothing else than a part of the strategy to be used by Muslims to take over the rest of the world and convert all peoples to Islam.

It's "al-Taqiyya", or deception, the Islamic word for concealing or disguising one's beliefs, convictions, ideas, feelings, opinions, and/or strategies.

It is impossible to understand Islam and Muslims by listening to their protestations against terror and their proclamations of patriotism for America. Usually, it is wise and fair to give people the benefit of the doubt but when it comes to national safety and the future of America, we had better look twice, even thrice at Muslim patriotism. Why? Because Islam permits lying! It is called "Al-taqiyya." One Muslim said that Al-taqiyya means dissimulation then he expanded it to diplomacy but he should have gone further to deception. Now some Muslims who do not follow the Quran are as faithful Americans as any of us, but the problem is, we cannot know.

As Mona Walter, a Somali ex-Muslim living in Sweden, said during a May 2, 2015 interview, "*Muslims are normally good people like everyone else. But then when they read the Quran, then they become a killing machine.*"

http://pamelageller.com/2015/05/muslim-read-quran-left-islam.html/

Muslims lie when it is in their interest to do so and "Allah" will not hold them accountable for lying when it is beneficial to the cause of Islam. They can lie without any guilt or fear of accountability or retribution. A lie in the defense of Islam is approved even applauded in their "holy" books. Muslims are permitted to lie: (1) to save their lives, (2) to reconcile a husband and wife, (3) to persuade a woman into a bedroom, and (4) to facilitate one on his journey. Muslims are even permitted to disavow Islam and Muhammad if it is not a genuine heart-felt rejection. Muslims will tell you that concealment of a truth is not an abandonment of that truth if it benefits Islam.

Unlike Christians who are saved once for all by the grace of God through faith in Christ's propitiatory death, no Muslim knows for sure if his works are good enough for Heaven. The only Muslim who knows for sure that his eternal destiny is secure and he will drop into a delightful garden filled with 72 virgins on soft green cushions is the one who dies while "taking out" unbelievers in Islam.

Most Muslims will not have the "opportunity" to become a martyr in this war between Islam and the rest of the world; and make no mistake every true Muslim must be involved in making America (or the nation where he lives) a Muslim nation. Since Muslims are limited in their ability to die for the cause, they can help the cause by supporting terrorists with money, and cover. Sure, they are aiding terror against the U.S. but since they believe they are doing Allah's will, then any deception is acceptable.

How should this affect America's war on terror? Officials must look closely at every Muslim chaplain in the military and in our prisons; also look at those involved in the CIA, FBI, and other sensitive areas; look at all Arabic translators, military or civilian; look at all Muslim employees at the Pentagon, White House, atomic power plants, and in Congress; look at all civilian Muslim pilots; look at Muslim clerics in all U.S. mosques. In other words, get serious about this war before our cities are rubble.

So… we are at war and it's called "Jihad", the Holy war by Islam to take over the rest of the world as such is its mission given by God. "*I don't think you can overstate the importance that the rise of Islamic Fundamentalism will have to the rest of the world in the century ahead –especially if, as seems possible, its most fanatical elements get their hands on nuclear and chemical weapons and the means to deliver them against their enemies.*" (Ronald Reagan).

By those that practice it, it is called a "*religion of peace*".

There are those, however, who would disagree with that statement. Some people see the Muslims as an angry, violent people who use the two-fold method of Jihad and Fatah *(a Palestinian terrorist organization)* to further their geo-political plans, and sadly, the vast majority of people both here in America and abroad, remain blissfully ignorant of the ever-swelling tide of Muslim cultural expansion.

In Washington, DC, there is a group known as **As-Sabiqun**, and it's leader is **Imam Abdul Alim Musa,** (born 1945 as Clarence Reams), a Muslim American activist - His plans and goals are those of most Muslims living both here in the US and in Europe, "*We resolve to utilize all the tools of Islam to develop an analysis and plan of action to totally and completely obliterate the hold of jahiliyyah* (the state of ignorance of the guidance from God) *and enable Islam to take complete control of our lives, and ultimately, the lives of all human beings on Earth.*"

"*The whole world must submit to Islam, Kafirs are the enemy simply by not being Muslims. Violence and terror are made sacred by the Quran. Peace comes only with submission to Islam.*" (*"Sharia Law for Non-Muslims"* by Bill Warner)

Bukhari 4,52,142 – *Muhammad said, " To battle Kafirs in jihad for even one day is greater than the entire earth and everything on it. A spot in Paradise smaller than your riding crop is greater than the entire earth and everything on it. A day or a night's travel in jihad is greater than the entire world and everything on it. "*

The three stages of Jihad

1- **Stealth Jihad,** or preparation stage. In other words: al-Taqiyya.

This stage is when the Muslims are still a minority in any non-Islamic country. They make preparation in every area from financial to physical, to military, etc.

Quran, Surat 8:59 – *"And let not those who disbelieve think they will escape. Indeed, they will not cause failure [to Allah]."*

Quran, Surat 8:60 – *"And prepare against them whatever you are able of power and of steeds of war by which you may terrify the enemy of Allah and your enemy and others besides them whom you do not know [but] whom Allah knows. And whatever you spend in the cause of Allah will be fully repaid to you, and you will not be wronged."*

2- **Active Jihad**, which occurs when Muslims are a minority with strength, influence and power.

During this stage, active Muslims (usually called "terrorists", "Jihadists", "Salafists", etc. by the media) start murdering, killing, bombing and others acts of war, individually or in groups.

Quran, Surat 9:4 – *"If the idol worshipers sign a peace treaty with you, and do not violate it, nor band together with others against you, you shall fulfill your treaty with them until the expiration date. God loves the righteous."*

Quran, Surat 9:5 – *"And when the sacred months have passed, then kill the polytheists wherever you find them and capture them and besiege them and sit in wait for them at every place of ambush. But if they should repent, establish prayer, and give zakah (a type of worship of self-purification), let them [go] on their way. Indeed, Allah is Forgiving and Merciful."*

3- **Global Jihad** - or war against the Kafirs to establish Islam around the globe. Jihad is a political system with a religious motivation.

In May 1998 Jonathan Miller, then a reporter with ABC News, interviewed Bin Laden, who believed that he was a servant of Allah and that his primary mission was to spread by fighting for the religion of light, "*I am one of the servants of Allah. We do our duty of fighting for the sake of the religion of Allah. It is also our duty to send a call to all the people of the world to enjoy this great light and to embrace Islam and experience the happiness in Islam. Our primary mission is nothing but the furthering of this religion...*

Quran, Surat 9:14 – *"You shall fight them (the nonbelievers), for God will punish them at your hands, humiliate them, grant you victory over them, and cool the chests of the believers."*

Quran, Surat 9:32 – *"They want to extinguish the light of Allah with their mouths, but Allah refuses except to perfect His light, although the disbelievers dislike it."*

Quran, Surat 9:33 – *"It is He who has sent His Messenger with guidance and the religion of truth to manifest it over all religion, although they who associate others with Allah dislike it."*

Jihad is an obligation. However when enough people perform it, it is no longer obligatory upon others.

Quran, Surat 4:95 – *"Believers who stay at home in safety, other than those who are disabled, are not equal to those who fight with their wealth and their lives for Allah's cause [jihad]."*

Bukhari 4,52,96 – *"Muhammad said: "Anyone who arms a jihadist is rewarded just as a fighter would be; anyone who gives proper care to a holy warrior's dependents is rewarded just as a fighter would be."*

World Domination is part of the *Daru 'l-Harb doctrine* of Islam. This Doctrine comes out of verses in the Quran which say that the ***world belongs to Allah***. There are also Hadiths which say it. Most Muslims take this as meaning that the entire world must be converted to Islam.

Note: Definition of the Daru 'l-Harb doctrine: DARU 'L-HARB, *"The land of warfare."* According to the Dictionary Ghiyasu 'l-Lughat Daru 'l-harb is *"a country belonging to the infidels which has not been subdued by Islam."* According to the Qamus, it is *"a country in which peace has not been proclaimed between Muslims and unbelievers."*

Quran, Surat 22:64 – *"To Him belongs what is in the heavens and what is on the earth. And indeed, Allah is the Free of need, the Praiseworthy."*

Quran, Surat 22:65 – *"Do you not see that Allah has subjected to you whatever is on the earth and the ships which run through the sea by His command? And He restrains the sky* *from falling upon the earth, unless by His permission. Indeed Allah, to the people, is Kind and Merciful."*

Quran, Surat 31:26 – *"To Allah belongs all that is in the heavens and the earth. He is the Rich, the Praised."*

Quran, Surat 2:218 – *"And those who emigrated for the cause of Allah and then were killed or died - Allah will surely provide for them a good provision. And indeed, it is Allah who is the best of providers."*

Quran, Surat 22:78 (extract) – **"***You shall strive for the cause of Allah as you should strive for His cause. He has chosen you and has placed no hardship on you in practicing your religion."*

Since the world belongs to Allah, any power that prevents Muslims from having it is by definition oppressive, and usurping the Umma's rights. *("Umma" means "Nation" or "Community"; in this context: "Islamic Nation" or "Islamic Community".)*

Sharia, the Quranic law, through Jihad, claims political supremacy over the Constitution of the United States. Although the Sharia violates every principle of our Constitution, it is being implemented today, because Americans are unaware about its meaning.

The Sharia lays out the complete process and strategy of immigration into a Kafir nation and what to do to islamicize the society.

When Muslims first arrive, they accept their new home and announce that Islam is a brother religion to Christianity and

Judaism. After these claims are in place and accepted come the demands for changes in the Kafir nation. Those who resist these changes are called bigots, islamophobes and racists, even though it is never made clear why resisting Political Islam has anything to do with race.

In conclusion, Jihad means war against Kafirs to establish Islam.

Quran, Surat 2:216 – *"You are commanded to fight although you dislike it. You may hate something that is good for you, and love something that is bad for you. Allah knows and you do not."*

Quran, Surat 4:89 – *"They would have you become Kafirs like them so you will all be the same. Therefore, do not take any of them as friends until they have abandoned their homes to fight for Allah's cause (jihad). But if they turn back, find them and kill them wherever they are."*

Question: Is there any Court of Law in America who would judge the above Surats compatible with the Constitution and Law of the United States of America?

Rules of Jihad have been described in "*Management of Savagery*", one of the most prominent books on Jihad written by an unknown Jihad ideologist around 2004, Abu Bakr Naji. A lot of the guidelines for Jihad seem to form a source of inspiration for the Islamic State about a decade later.

Management of Savagery discusses the need to create and manage nationalist and religious resentment and violence in order to create long-term propaganda opportunities for jihadist groups. Notably, Naji discusses the value of provoking military responses from superpowers in order to recruit and train guerilla fighters and to create martyrs. Naji suggests that a long-lasting strategy of attrition will reveal fundamental weaknesses in the ability of superpowers to defeat committed jihadists.

One suggestion by Naji is, first, to kill all non-Muslims politicians in order to replace them with Muslims politicians who will take charge of the people.

(English translation of "Management of Savagery" by William McCants, May 23, 2006)

https://azelin.files.wordpress.com/2010/08/abu-bakr-naji-the-management-of-savagery-the-most-critical-stage-through-which-the-umma-will-pass.pdf

Here is another Jihad veteran: **Abu Musab al-Souri**.

Moustapha Sitt Mariam Nassar, his true name, born in Aleppo, Syria, in 1958, advocates a local Jihad that is inexpensive but efficient. Merah, Tsarnaev, Adebolajo, Fort Hood, Toulouse, Boston, London, Sand Bernardino, Paris, Orlando, Nice, Berlin, London, Barcelona... the killings perpetrated by young men are repeated all over the world. No more simultaneous bombings in subways and train stations. No more planes hijacked or launched on towers. No more attacks requiring years of meticulous preparation and sophisticated networks.

Recent jihadist attacks in the West possess a new logic. They are executed by tiny autonomous cells acting with whatever means are at their disposal. This is the "new jihad," theorized by this Hispano-Syrian, whose effects are particularly perverse.

René d'Armor

Epilogue

Today, the United States faces what is the most insidious ideological threat: the totalitarian socio-political doctrine that Islam calls Sharia.

America's national security is at stake and, by extension, the security of all democratic Western countries.

Unlike common law, Sharia is not interpretative, nor can it be changed. There is no Golden Rule.

"The Quran and the Islamic law, Sharia, are Anti-constitutional and reject:

a. The bedrock proposition that the government have a right to make law for themselves;

b. The republican democracy governed by the Constitution;

c. Freedom of conscience; individual liberty (including in matters of personal privacy and sexual preference);

d. Freedom of expression (including the liberty to analyze and criticize the Sharia);

e. Economic liberty (including private property);

f. Equal treatment under the law (including that of men and women, and of Muslims and Non-Muslims);

g. Freedom from cruel and unusual punishments; an unequivocal condemnation of terrorism (i.e., one that is based on a common sense meaning of the term and does not rationalize barbarity as legitimate "resistance"); and

h. An abiding commitment to deflate and resolve political controversies by the ordinary mechanisms of federalism and democracy, not wanton violence."

("Sharia: The Threat to America" – Download from http://shariahthethreat.org/)

From *"Sharia Law for Non-Muslims"* by **Bill Warner**: *"When you study Islam in Europe today (*with more or less 50,000,000 Muslims), *you are seeing America in 20 years (maybe a lot less...). Why? The actions by Muslims in Europe are based on Sharia law, the same Sharia law that is beginning to be implemented in America today."*

- The September 11, 2001 attack was a political action motivated by a religious mandate for endless jihad.

- Textbooks in America must be approved by Islamic councils.

- American employers and schools are met with demands for time and space to do Islamic prayer.

- Etc… etc…The list is long and all these demands are in accordance with Sharia law.

URGENT ACTIONS

1) The Anti-constitutional Quran and Sharia must be made illegal in the United States of America.

<u>Article 6 of the US Constitution</u> should suffice to make it so:

"This Constitution, and the Laws of the United States which shall be made in Pursuance thereof; and all Treaties made, or which shall be made, under the Authority of the United States, shall be the supreme Law of the Land; and the Judges in every State shall be bound thereby, any Thing in the Constitution or Laws of any State to the Contrary notwithstanding."

2) People who want to live under the Islamic law (Sharia) must not be allowed to stay nor to enter the United States of America

This is not "Un-American," dumb, stupid, reckless, dangerous and racist. Congressmen and Senators swore that they would never allow such legislation to stop Muslims to immigrate in the U.S.A., and president Obama called such a prohibition on immigration unconstitutional when presidential candidate, Donald Trump, in 2016, suggested that the U.S. should limit or temporarily suspend the immigration of certain ethnic groups, nationalities, and even people of certain religions (Muslims).

Well, "Surprise, Surprise!!!" It seems that the selective immigration ban is already law and has been applied on several occasions. Created by McCarran and Walter, two Democrats, and known as the McCarran-Walter Act, the Immigration and Nationality Act of 1952 allows for the "*Suspension of entry or imposition of restrictions by president. Whenever the president finds that the entry of aliens or of any class of aliens into the United States would be detrimental to the interests of the United States, the president may, by proclamation, and for such period as he shall deem necessary, suspend the entry of all aliens or any class of aliens as immigrants or non-immigrants or impose on the entry of aliens any restrictions he may deem to be appropriate."*

The act was utilized by President Jimmy Carter, no less, in 1979 to keep Iranians out of the United States, but he actually did more. He made all Iranian students already here check in, and then he deported a bunch. Seven thousand were found in violation of their visas, 15,000 Iranians were forced to leave the United States in 1979.

It is of note that the act requires that an applicant for immigration must be of good moral character and "attached to the principles of the Constitution."

Since the Quran forbids Muslims to swear allegiance to the U.S. Constitution, technically, all Muslims should be refused immigration.

Authenticated at:
http://library.uwb.edu/static/USimmigration/1952_immigration_and_nationality_act.html

www.ingramcontent.com/pod-product-compliance
Lightning Source LLC
LaVergne TN
LVHW021614080426
835510LV00019B/2563